COMPASSIONATE COUNSELING

Jay E. Adams

Institute for Nouthetic Studies, a ministry of Mid-America Baptist Theological Seminary, 2095 Appling Road, Memphis, TN 38016
mabts.edu and nouthetic.org

Compassionate Counseling
by Jay E. Adams
Copyright © 2024 by the Institute for Nouthetic Studies,
© 2007 by Jay E. Adams

New Testament quotations are from the Christian Counselor's New Testament and Proverbs Copyright © 2019 by the Institute for Nouthetic Studies, 1977, 1980, 1994, 2000 by Jay E. Adams

All Old Testament quotation are taken from the New American Standard Bible, © 1995 by The Lockman Foundation.

ISBN: 978-1-949737-72-1 (Print)
ISBN: 978-1-949737-73-8 (eBook)
Old ISBN: 978-1-889032-59-7

Editor: Donn R. Arms
Design: James Wendorf | www.FaithfulLifePublishers.com

Library of Congress Cataloging-in-Publication Data
Names: Adams, Jay E., 1929 - 2020
Title: Compassionate Counseling
Jay E. Adams
Description: Memphis: Institute for Nouthetic Studies, 2024
Identifiers: ISBN 9781949737721 (paper)
Classification: LCC BV4012.2 .A33 | DDC 253.5

All rights reserved. No part of this publication may be reproduced, stored in a retrieval system, or transmitted in any form or by any means – electronic, mechanical, photocopy, recording, or any other – except for brief quotations in printed reviews, without prior permission of the publisher.

Published in the United States of America

Contents

1. Compassionate Counseling — 1
2. Compassion is Needed — 5
3. A Case in Point — 9
4. Compassion, Sympathy, and Empathy — 13
5. One Form Compassion May Take — 17
6. Compassion is Not Acceptance — 21
7. Compassionate Teaching — 27
8. Another Side to Compassion in Teaching — 31
9. Are You Moved? — 35
10. "How Do I Get it?" — 39
11. Jesus' Compassion — 43
12. Compassion isn't Optional — 49
13. The Good Samaritan — 53
14. Compassion in Conflict — 57
15. Philemon's Compassion — 61
16. How God Uses Compassion — 65
17. When Compassion is Wrong — 69
18. When Compassion is Withheld — 73
19. Compassion for Those Who Minister — 77
20. Compassion for Brothers in Extremities — 81
21. The Cost of Compassion — 85
22. Compassion for Animals? — 91
23. What Compassion Does for Counseling — 93

CHAPTER ONE

Compassionate Counseling

Introduction

Granted, the Scriptures say little directly about counseling with compassion. There is, however, a considerable amount about compassion in them (especially about God's compassion toward us). But inasmuch as counseling has to do with helping those in need – of one sort or another – compassion is more than a secondary concern to a biblical counselor because of the work he does. If counseling means honoring God by helping people find His solutions to their problems (and it does), then the biblical material about compassion bears directly upon the task of one who longs to meet that need. Passages having to do with compassion generally, then, may rightly be applied to the ways in which counselors relate to their counselees. What is true of normal relationships cannot be of any less importance to those involved in the intensity of the counseling milieu.

Because so little has been written about compassion in counseling, I have undertaken to fill the gap.[1] Since compassion is an essential component of all truly biblical counseling, it is essential to understand its nature, place, and effects upon counselees, counselors, and the counseling that they engage in. And in addition to filling a gap, I also recognize the importance of setting the record straight. For whatever reasons – misunderstandings, malicious misrepresentation, or something else – in some circles Nouthetic counseling has gotten a bad rap. Its proponents have been characterized as callous, cold, austere, and legalistic. In fact, nothing could be farther from the truth. And, in this volume, I intend to demonstrate that fact. Since biblical counselors don't make a living off of their counseling, but freely give their time and effort out of

---

1. You can read through the indices of book after book – even those about biblical counseling – and find no reference to compassion.

concern for others, you can see right off that there must be something wrong with that analysis (especially when made by those who do charge fees for their counsel). To picture Nouthetic counselors as hawks circling overhead looking for some poor Christian to pounce upon in order to rip him apart, is nothing short of ridiculous (if not scandalous). Like so many others, they too could refer those in need to nonbiblical counselors while remaining at home watching their favorite ball team on television.

Indeed, even more basic is the fact that Nouthetic Counselors earnestly desire to see God glorified by the changes that the ministry of His Word brings about in the lives of persons caught in the webs of sin. To help them disentangle themselves from their predicaments in ways that please God is such a counselor's overriding motivation. But to please Him, the counselor must show compassion. That's so, as you will see, because God demands it. It's possible to say and do many of the things God requires according to scriptural guidelines – even to help people (if God blesses His Word in spite of the fact) – without an ounce of compassion. But that isn't Nouthetic Counseling. It is but a poor substitute for it.

Nouthetic counselors have always emphasized the vertical dimension in counseling as well as the horizontal one. So if one's heart is not right toward God, whatever he does in His Name displeases Him. That is why Nouthetic counselors make it a practice to *focus* not upon principles and techniques, but upon their own (and their counselee's) relation to God. That is not to say that they neglect biblical principles and practices. Far from it! But they do not consider them of overriding importance. They recognize that, above all else, they must counsel in God's presence in ways that honor Him. And one of those ways – every bit as significant as any other counseling principle – is by showing compassion toward counselees. It will, therefore, be a central concern of this book to search the biblical record to discover what compassion is, the place it ought to have in counseling, and how it is to be shown to others.

Let it be said at the outset, however, that compassion is not some cheap substitute for genuine biblical counsel. True compassion involves taking the time to learn what God has to say about human difficulties and how He expects us to confront them. It means working long and hard with counselees – some of whom are not always too cooperative. In no way, then, can one expect to please God by engaging in "sloppy agape" (as someone appropriately dubbed emotional substitutes for true compassion). Principles and practices must be thoroughly biblical, fully learned, and carefully followed in the ways that God has prescribed. But in doing so, people suffering from the ravages of sin upon their lives must be confronted compassionately. Counseling, then, must not be done in a cold, mechanical, white-coated manner. The biblical counselor should "rejoice with those who rejoice and weep with those who weep" (Romans 12:15). He should become compassionately involved!

So much for preliminaries. We shall now turn to the study that lies before us. But as we do so, let it also be known that compassion for another can be studied, understood, encouraged, directed and the like, but cannot be generated. This book has no such power to do this for you. Yet in ancillary ways, it is my hope that it may *assist* in bringing about that inner visceral concern for others that insists upon helping them. If it does so, it will be by setting forth the picture of sin and misery that God describes in His Word together with the remarkable manner in which God has shown compassion upon human beings by providing a way out of their misery (cf. I Corinthians 10:13). Having said that, let's turn to the next chapter, where we shall explore the need for compassion.

CHAPTER TWO
Compassion is Needed

To see the hurt in the bloodshot eyes of a wife who has just discovered her husband's infidelity, to hear the fear in the poorly modulated voices of parents whose boy was arrested for drug trafficking, and to see the anger in the inflamed face of a pastor who has just been fired for preaching truth, is to know something of what a counselor encounters from day to day. The counselor sees the ravages of sin upon bodies, learns more than he wants to know about the utter destruction of once-promising marriages, feels deeply in his gut something of the turmoil and heartache of ruined relationships, and enters into the hardships of a husband diagnosed with MS. He is privy to all of the sadnesses, horrors, pains, embarrassments, aberrations, anxieties, and despairs that plague a race of men under a divine curse. He must console the one who has lost his child due to the recklessness of a drunken driver. He mourns along with the mother whose son has been killed at war. He helps make sense of seemingly confused events that occur under the rule of divine sovereignty. Daily he faces greedy, self-centered whiners who expect the world to treat them as if they were God's gift to mankind but have discovered that others think differently. He intervenes when two bitter members of his congregation become estranged over a business deal gone sour. He listens patiently when people doubt the goodness of God, when they question the validity of the church, when they justify their backsliding ways, and he deals with them patiently. In it all he tries, like God, to remember that men like himself are "only flesh" (Psalm 78:39).

A faithful biblical counselor handles objections firmly but gently. He remembers Jesus' words in Luke 6:26, "Be merciful as your Father is merciful." But he also recognizes the futility of helping those who stubbornly reject the truth and pleads with them to think again. He believes in the hard and often thankless task of pursuing church discipline when called for –

and does so for the sake of God's Name, the benefit of His church, and the reclamation of the recalcitrant sinner. He continues to help even when subjected to volumes of misguided abuse streaming from the mouths of self-justifying sinners who don't want to own up to the truth. Rather than give up on them, he encourages those who fall again and again, and seeks to strengthen them for the future. He is exposed to the filth and grime of sin on every hand. He sees it, hears it, experiences it – firsthand. Sex, crime, hatred, envy, avarice – he is familiar with the wicked ways that proceed from the human heart. And how does he respond to all of this? How is he able to keep his composure – not to say sanity – in the wake of it? By compassion; by showing compassion to saint and sinner alike.

But what quality is found in compassion that explains why a counselor doesn't become disillusioned? In what salutary ways does compassion enter into the counseling of men and women with so many needs? I shall enlarge upon this matter in later chapters.

For now, from another angle, consider the plight of those who, as Solomon put it, are caught in the cords of their own sin (cf. Proverbs 5:22). Four such typical circumstances come to mind. First, sitting in shame, are those who dreamed of fame and fortune in their future and have now grown old without either. They are savvy enough to recognize that they spent their lives waiting for their ship to come in only to discover that, if there ever was such a vessel, it was lost at sea. They oriented their lives around a fantasy. Now, they have nothing. They are bitter, resentful – people to be pitied. What do they need? Among other things, compassion.

Second, consider also those who for years lived lives of lies. They lied about their achievements, about their failures – indeed, about anything they thought might be to their advantage. Now, their lies have caught up with them. They have been found out. People no longer believe or trust them. Former friends shy away from them, and they are left alone with their lies. They are empty, vacuous people who desperately need genuine, biblical compassion.

Ponder yet another scenario. Consider defeated, disillusioned, disheartened persons who throughout life ran from problems. They ran from jobs, from marriages, from churches. Whenever things became at all difficult, they ran. But now, there is no place left to which to run. Their backs are against the wall; there is no escape, they can run no longer – they have been caught! Now, they are out of breath from running! Because it is likely that they will attempt to run from counseling too, they must be shown compassion.

Take a glimpse at one more situation. Meet the excuse-making blame-shifter. Everything bad that ever happened to him was someone else's fault. If he had only done his part, why then, he would have succeeded and would not have ended up the miserable wreck of humanity he now is. He blames his wife, his boss, his pastor and elders, and (though he may be loathe to admit it) he blames God. He doesn't even have a good word for his faithful dog! What shall we say of this faultfinding, complaining soul who is so unpleasant to be around? Just this – he needs Nouthetic compassion!

People we counsel are afflicted, distressed, worried, sick, friendless, uncomfortable, crushed, suffering, sorrowful, sad, heartbroken, small, petty, contemptible, mean, venal, covetous, and the like – and they are all in need of compassion. Some have been abused, attacked, hounded, ill-treated, defamed, reproached, maltreated, misused, oppressed, slandered, vilified; and they are miserable. But sadly, they don't know that these things are not really their problem. Certainly many, who have not brought these wrongs upon themselves, need to be pitied. Yet the fundamental problem, in each case, is not the wrong done to them but their failure to respond to wrong rightly – that is to say, biblically. Instead, by responding some other way, they have compounded and complicated their difficulties. They tell themselves, "I've got problems," not realizing that their problems have them! As a result, many of them live the melancholy lives of victims rather than the joyful lives of victors. Such people clearly need compassionate counseling!

But that isn't all. Those well-meaning, but ill-instructed or duped individuals who are caught up in liberal, cultic, or unorthodox churches, who have been led to believe errors that, when followed, lead to disillusionment and despair, need compassion. When Jesus saw that the crowd was like sheep without a true shepherd, we read that "He…had compassion on them…and began to teach them many things" (Mark 6:34). The welfare of God's flock has been sorely neglected by many so-called pastors; and the flock has even been fleeced by some that are actually wolves in shepherd's clothing. Falsehood – leading to shoddy living – abounds in the church, on "Christian" radio and TV, and within the covers of many religious books. How sorely do persons entangled in such sub-Christian milieus need compassionate, shepherdly instruction!

After reading this chapter, you may say to me, "It looks like you think that everyone who comes for counseling needs compassionate treatment." You've got it! That's just about so. Of course, there are those who come simply for information or to bounce ideas off another person. But even so, they also often need compassion in their struggles to comprehend data or make God-honoring decisions.

"Well," you say, "if compassion is so vital as you are saying, please tell me what it is and how I can get it."

All in good time.

CHAPTER THREE
A Case in Point

In the Introduction I noted that compassion does not often appear in counseling contexts, even in Scripture. But there are exceptions. I shall begin our present discussion by briefly considering a passage that plainly ties the two together. It is Jude 22–23:

> Show mercy to doubters, save others by pulling them out of the fire, and show mercy to others, with caution, hating even the clothing spotted by their flesh.

In those two verses are directions for counseling several sorts of persons in trouble which include showing mercy to them.

Consistent with his penchant for groups of three (evidenced throughout this letter), Jude mentions three sorts of believers who need "mercy." First, there are the doubters. Then, there are those who, finding themselves trapped in a fire, must be snatched out. Finally, as Jude shifts figures, the third sort is described as those with a loathsome disease by which a counselor might become infected if he doesn't take extreme precautions when helping them. Note, particularly, that these people need mercy.

In Jude we read that libertine heretics, about whom Peter warned in his second epistle, had succeeded in penetrating the church (Jude 4; II Peter 2:1–3, 12–22). Obviously, Peter's warnings were disregarded. Some church members had succumbed to their nefarious teaching by engaging in various sorts of debauchery, others were in the process of becoming involved, and a third group was in doubt about whether or not they should join the rest. Accordingly, in inverse order, these three groups correspond to the three states Jude describes in the verses quoted. Notice, again, God directs those who minister to them to "show mercy" in doing it.

Mercy is a prime element in compassion. Jude's word *eleeo* may be translated "to show mercy to, to have pity on" or even "to be compassionate toward." In addition to other uses, in the Septuagint,[1] it is also used to translate the Hebrew word for compassion.

Obviously, doubters, persons on the brink of destruction, and those who are spiritually ill with error must be pitied and shown merciful compassion. They are in grave danger. The urgency and depth of need pictured by Jude's vivid images emphasize that fact. As we have seen, mercy is the operative word in Jude 22–23. But what is the relationship between these three visceral terms, pity, mercy and compassion? It seems to be as follows: *pity* is the feeling one senses upon recognizing the plight of another. When full-blown, it develops into an attitude of tender good will, even toward such self-inflicted sufferers as those Jude mentions. It is this good will toward others in trouble that we call *mercy*. This, in turn, may lead to efforts made on behalf of the one in need, designed to ameliorate his suffering. Those efforts may be called *showing compassion upon*.

Now, these distinctions are somewhat arbitrary since, in biblical usage, each of the three terms blends with the other two as raindrops on the windshield run into one another. Consequently, while largely adhering to the distinctions just made, I shall not do so in a hard-and-fast manner in this book. One or another term may predominate in a particular discussion as a matter of emphasis in succeeding chapters. I want to lay emphasis, therefore, upon the word "emphasis." Let it suffice, then, to say that compassion is not compassion unless, in one way or another, it includes the qualities of pity and mercy.

That doubters – those considering the validity of some erroneous and degrading teaching – need our mercy ought to obvious. Yet I have known Christians to respond to their doubting brothers or sisters as if they had been recently handling a rancid fish. They seem not to be able to withdraw from them quickly enough! As Jude indicates, these sinners need

---

1. The Greek translation of the Old Testament.

A Case in Point

other believers to take the time and make the effort to engage them in kind discussion about their doubts. Surely, there is something incongruous, to say the least, about a sign posted at the gate of an estate just outside of Baltimore that reads:

> Sisters of Mercy
>
> Trespassers will be prosecuted
> to the full extent of the law

Enough said!

Those who find themselves a part of some deception that burns like fire all around them, who perhaps don't know which way to turn, need mercy shown to them. This ought to be obvious from Jude's powerful metaphor of being caught in a burning building. As Jude indicates, rather than dawdling, you must do something – even of a violent or radical nature – to rescue them. They must be "snatched" from the fire before they are destroyed by it!

Those who have been indulging in the debauchery of some heresy like that which Jude describes in verse 4 desperately need mercy as well. But the Christian who reaches out to help must take care not to become infected by it. Let him listen to the words of Alexander Pope:

> Vice is a monster of so frightful mien
> As to be hated needs but to be seen;
> Yet seen too oft, familiar with her face,
> We first endure, then pity, then embrace.

That must not happen, Jude says. People infected with sin need mercy; and the one who helps them needs wisdom and courage. But he also must take care. There are so few who seem to want to help those who have become involved in degrading sinful behavior, but the church cannot simply throw them to the wolves. Pastors need to consider such matters, preach about them, and encourage their members to help those among them who, in one way or another, need compassion.

CHAPTER FOUR
Compassion, Sympathy, and Empathy

The word "compassion" comes into English from the Latin words "suffer" and "with," and is the exact equivalent to the Greek-derived term "sympathy." Both words, according to their etymology, carry the idea of suffering or experiencing together with another what he is feeling. They have to do with physical responses to trouble, particularly those related to the viscera. To have compassion for another, in this sense, means, literally, to so enter into his experience that one feels what he feels, suffers what he suffers.

But the etymology of words rarely does more than give hints and clues to their present meanings. Hence, while sympathy has retained much of its original meaning, compassion has evolved into a fuller, richer term. While sympathy still carries the idea of experiencing the same thing as another, compassion goes one step further as it often expresses not only the desire to help, but also the act of helping one who is afflicted. Good will is transmuted into merciful actions. That is why, when Jesus saw the multitudes as sheep without a shepherd, He was "moved" with compassion to "teach them many things" (John 6:34). Inner feelings of sympathy and pity so dominated Him that they moved Him to action. Jude's use of "mercy" in reference to persons being adversely influenced by hurtful teaching was more than deep feelings of pity. It was more than suffering along with them. It was concern leading to action calculated to block all further detrimental influence and to extricate those who had already fallen prey to it. In biblical cases, then, to be compassionate means more than to exude sympathy. It means to *show* mercy to the one in need.

What about "empathy"? Doesn't the word imply something greater than sympathy? Certainly. The term does not appear in the Greek New Testament, but it is an integral part of the English semantic territory that we are traversing. According to its derivation, it means to "enter into" the suffering that another experiences. Whereas sympathy pictures someone standing by another who suffers, to some extent "feeling his pain" from without, empathy envisions someone actually stepping into the same suffering in such a way that it allows him greater understanding of and participation in the experience.

Well, then, is empathy the same as compassion? No. In empathy, one may more fully enter into another's experience, but he does so no more than the suffering one does himself. He experiences the ordeal precisely as the sufferer does. He takes on feelings and views of what is happening that coincide with those of the one undergoing the experience. Of course, no one is really able to fully empathize with another, as Proverbs 14:10 makes clear: "The heart knows its own bitterness, and a stranger does not share its joy." Yet empathy, to the extent that it is possible, views things as another does. Is empathy the same as compassion then? No, I repeat. Why not? For the following two reasons: 1) empathy, though signifying one's deeper involvement than in sympathy, at best fails to enter into the other person's problem fully enough; and 2) empathy fails to do anything to diminish the sufferer's problem. Compassion, on the other hand, moves one to action. It does not allow him to stand by, as sympathy does. Nor does it sanction mere entrance into a problem in some deeper way. Rather, it moves one to become so involved that he seeks to find God's remedy to the problem and will not rest until he does so. In other words, compassion is becoming so involved with the other person that one not only feels his pain, but also proceeds to do something about it. Compassion, therefore, enters into a problem more deeply than the sufferer himself. The latter feels, suffers, agonizes; compassion moves beyond the suffering to God's way of dealing with it. A compassionate person will settle neither for sympathizing groans and sighs nor for empathetic understanding and agreement. He says that he feels the sharpness of the pain and agrees that it is serious, but then goes on to add that all-important word "but..." The compassionate person is a counselor at heart. He

Compassion, Sympathy, and Empathy

will not allow a problem to remain unsettled as he stands by. He will see more deeply into it than the sufferer. He will find God's solution to it. "Yes," he says, "I fully agree with you that your problem is acute, and to the extent that it is possible to do so, I feel something of what you feel, but...." It is that "but," remember, that makes all the difference between compassion on the one hand and sympathy and empathy on the other. No counseling is envisioned in sympathy or empathy. The "but" of compassion signals the possibility of solving the problem through ministering God's counsel. Jesus and Jude showed compassion for others, not mere sympathy or empathy.

Chapter Five
One Form Compassion May Take

We have seen that compassion is emotionally charged action taken by one person in behalf of another who is in trouble. But it is not simply action; for a Christian counselor the action must be in accord with biblical principles appropriate to the situation and to the problem addressed. What does that look like? In the following example, you will see only one form that compassion might take.

Return, for the moment, to the case of a Christian who has spent the lion's share of his life waiting for a shipment of gold to make it into port. He is embittered, lonely, frustrated, and ashamed. His aimless, fruitless lifestyle has intensified his difficulties. He has finally awakened to the enormity of his failure. Neither fame nor fortune is possible now that he has grown old. Were they to come at this last hour, he would have little time or energy left to enjoy them. He, therefore, sees no future; all there is to do is to await death.

In ferreting out these facts, the compassionate counselor will seek to understand something of the plight of his erring brother in order to enter into his circumstance as a participant who wishes not merely to experience it, but to radically change it. He, therefore, will seek first to frame the situation in biblical terms. In doing so, he may have recourse to Proverbs 11:7: "When a wicked person dies his expectations will perish, and the unjust person's hope of wealth will be lost." He wants his counselee to recognize himself as the one whose picture Solomon has taken and framed.

Perhaps the idea of his hope of wealth perishing with him will ring a bell with this counselee especially if he has reached the point of despairing of all fame or fortune. But as a Christian, though having led a largely worthless life, he may still object to being called "wicked" or "unjust." The counselor may find it necessary to explain that the sinful abuse of talents and opportunities granted him was indeed wicked before the Lord. He may need to persuade him from the Scriptures that it is fundamentally unjust to expect wealth and notoriety when he has given neither God nor others reason to grant them. He may have to spend time enforcing the truth that the description of the man in Proverbs is a portrait of him and the life he has led. In addition to the verse quoted, he may wish to draw further upon Proverbs, this time referring him to the following statement: "The desire of the lazy person kills him since his hands have refused to work" (Proverbs 21:25). His sinful expectations have, as we say today, "been the very death of him." These expectations are sinful because all along he has been depending upon receiving a windfall rather than fulfilling responsibilities and working hard at the tasks at hand.

You may ask, "But is showing a man his sin compassionate? Isn't that rubbing it in?" No, it isn't a lack of compassion to tell the truth from God's Word.

Was Jesus compassionate when He restored Peter by requiring him to reaffirm his love three times – once for each denial (John 21)? Yes. Didn't He "rub it in?" No, He didn't. Though Peter was crestfallen, he needed to know that he had been fully restored to discipleship upon acknowledgement of and repentance for his sin. This was Jesus' way of effecting that. In helping counselees, a counselor worth his salt will never pass by sin unnoticed because he wants to enable his counselee, like Peter, to put it behind him. Only by exposing and dealing with it can he get on with his life in a proper way. To ignore sin, then, would reveal a serious lack of compassion. Compassion, you see, is not all sweetness and light. Like the surgeon's knife, the compassionate counselor's words hurt in order to heal. That is true compassion!

Having succeeded in making his points (perhaps after a long, hard struggle), the counselor will go on to call his counselee to repentance for gross negligence of his God-given abilities and many missed opportunities to put them to work for Him. Following repentance, the counselor together with the counselee chart out the most expeditious route for the counselee to take in his remaining years, one that will grant him

One Form Compassion May Take

maximum opportunity to redeem the future. The counselor will show him how to lay up treasures in heaven and encourage him to do so that he may at last have a realistic expectation of true wealth in his future – a hope that will not perish with his demise, but will be realized in the very act of dying! Is that compassion? You'd better believe it!

There are many other forms that compassionate counseling may take, some of which will appear as we progress in understanding compassion at work in counseling. But in the one just sketched, the basic elements that apply to all stand out clearly:

1) A compassionate counselor must desire to fully and accurately assess a counselee's plight and a willingness to become emotionally moved to the point of taking biblical action to remedy it in ways that conform to biblical teaching;

2) This is followed by the determination to set forth an honest, biblical evaluation of the counselee's situation, even when it involves difficult things to say. This willingness to use the biblical knife is not only compassionate, it is absolutely necessary whenever repentance is a prerequisite to true, lasting, God-honoring change; and

3) Then, upon confession of sin and an expressed desire on the counselee's part to do whatever God requires of him, the two will work out the details of acquiring the new attitudes and taking the new actions that must replace the old ones.

In one way or another, these elements are foundational to biblical counseling. Of course, much is missing from this bare-bones description, but additional facts may be found elsewhere.[1]

So, of what does compassion consist? Surely, to sum it up, we may say that it consists of caring enough for people in trouble to go to great lengths to help them extricate themselves from that trouble in God's ways. Compassion, while having strong emotional content, is by no means devoid of

---

1. See, especially, *Critical Stages of Biblical Counseling* as well as my other standard texts on the subject.

the rest of those factors just mentioned. It includes courage to confront, willingness to say the hard things, desire to find God's will for one's counselee, and – most of all – a deep commitment to honoring God in all that transpires.

Chapter Six
Compassion is Not Acceptance

"I have been taught that Christians should be accepting people, and that acceptance – rather than judging others – is a means of showing compassion. Where have I gone wrong?"

Well, we do accept others, but not for what they are. God does not do so, nor should his people.[1] If God were to accept people apart from justification through the work and merits of Jesus Christ, that would make Jesus' death superfluous. The very fact that Jesus had to die for guilty sinners to *make* them acceptable to God and to His church is clear evidence of the fact that, apart from His atoning sacrifice, no one is acceptable.

Think about it. How could a holy God *accept* unholy sinners? In no other way than by the cleansing of Christ's blood could He do so. He is "of purer eyes than to behold iniquity" or to look on wickedness without judging it (Habakkuk 1:13). That is why Habakkuk was appalled at God's apparent indifference to the sins of the nation of Israel in his day. But in response to the prophet's questions about this, God assures him that it is only by faith that the righteous will live (Habakkuk 2:4). Apart from such faith, there is no hope. Indeed, He goes on to pronounce a series of "woes" against those who have not been justified by faith (vv. 8–19). Because God did not judge immediately, but would do so in His own time and way, Habakkuk had a hard time, imagining that God was allowing evil to go unjudged. But that was not the case. Habakkuk simply wanted to "jump the gun." God works according to His own schedule.

Because, as Habakkuk rightly says that God is of purer eyes than to behold evil without judging it, He could not accept people into His church, let alone into His heavenly kingdom, apart from justifying and changing them through

---

1. For instance, we read in Jeremiah 14:10 that "the Lord does not accept" His wandering sheep.

His Son. Divine holiness demands God's total separation from all evil and iniquity. The need, therefore, for forgiveness of sin and justification, in order to be accounted holy in His sight through the blood of Christ, shows unmistakably that the modern, non-Christian view of acceptance (which, tragically, some have brought into the church) is itself *un*acceptable. If God refuses to accept people as they are apart from Christ, the church must also do so.

"Well, I can see that, but isn't it unkind to demand redemptive change before accepting others?" Is, then, God unkind? Of course He isn't. The kindest thing one can do for another is to point out that he is unacceptable to God and, therefore, in need of a Savior. When a Christian fails to do so, he allows others to go on as if all were well with God when it is not. If unchecked by truth, such unenlightened behavior will lead to devastating consequences. No, it is acceptance that is unkind. It encourages falsehood. To allow a person to think he is right with God when he is not is one of the most unkind things one can do.

Jesus taught that only those who come to God His way are acceptable. The haughty guest who thought he could participate in the king's wedding feast was told that he could not do so (Matthew 22:11–14). People are unacceptable apart from the righteousness of Christ that, like the garment in the parable, must be graciously given by the King of Kings.

"I can see that. But what about accepting other Christians?" Of course, we must do so *in the Lord*. But even so, Christians are unacceptable as they are – *apart* from Him. The entire New Testament witnesses to that fact. Over and over again believers are exhorted to change. They are told that they must put off old unacceptable ways they have brought into their new life from the past, and that they must replace these with new ways acceptable to God. Why are we given all of the many directions for change if there is no need for it? Why put people out of the church when they stubbornly refuse to change? Why do New Testament writers insist on holiness (being set apart from sin to righteousness)?

Compassion is Not Acceptance

To what purpose did Christ send the sanctifying Spirit to dwell with His people?

No, acceptance is not compassionate. It is just the opposite. It misrepresents God, allows men to go on in ways unacceptable to Him, and thereby justifies their sin. It denies the need for a Savior and for a sanctifying Spirit. Acceptance and compassion are incompatible. Fewer doctrines that Christians have borrowed from the world are as blatantly non-Christian as this Gospel-denying one. Believers, therefore, must avoid using language which might imply that men may find acceptance apart from the redeeming work of Christ and the sanctifying work of the Holy Spirit.

Now, as for the possible comment about judging. Perhaps you have fallen prey to those who wrongly teach that Christians must never judge others. If such teaching were true, of course, it would follow that we should accept everyone. But it isn't true.

"Well, there's Matthew 7. Isn't that what Jesus taught there?"

Absolutely not.

"But it says 'don't judge.'"

Yes, but that isn't all. The Lord could not have been forbidding all judgment because He goes on to say that if you remove the log from your eye, then you will be able to remove the splinter from another's eye (v. 5). In order to do so, you must make a judgment about whose eye does or doesn't have a splinter before removing it! Moreover, when immediately thereafter He tells us not to throw pearls in front of swine or give what is holy to dogs (v. 6), Jesus certainly expects us to judge who is a dog or pig, doesn't He? Finally, in John 7:24, He plainly urges us to "make a right judgment."

No. It is impossible not to judge. One cannot avoid doing so. A person who doesn't judge actions of others is irresponsible. And as we have seen, he is unkind (even unloving) *because* he doesn't judge. What Jesus wants us to understand is that we shall be judged as we judge others. So He warns against the hypocrisy of finding minor faults in others when we refuse to eliminate worse sins in our own lives. The statement in John, moreover, indicates that there is such a thing as righteous judgment. It is that sort of judgment, one made after gathering all the facts (not one based on suspicion or insufficient evidence), that we should be careful to make. To obey this command from John we must make righteous judgments. Since we judge all of the time, we must not judge others in ways that we would not want to be judged. That is the import of Matthew 7.

Note

Approximately two weeks after writing the above, there appeared in our local paper an article by Billy Graham that exhibits the confused thinking and/or loose language that I am attempting to dispel. The title of the article is, "God accepts us just the way we are."[1] This banner headline, in itself, is extremely misleading. The article goes on to say, "One of the Bible's greatest truths is that when we turn in faith to Christ, God forgives us and accepts us just as we are." Further down in the article, Graham writes, "...we don't have to become perfect before He'll accept us..." Then, he explains, "God doesn't want us to remain spiritual infants..." That much, of course, is true. But, how do we grow up? He says, "One of the ways God has given...is through fellowship with other believers."

Now, let's analyze what he wrote. First, it is important to recognize that God does *not* "accept us just as we are." This is not a teaching of the Bible, let alone one of its "greatest truths." He accepts us only on the merits of Jesus Christ Who fulfilled all righteousness on behalf of God's elect. If we could be accepted as we are, why did Christ die? Second, we *must* become "perfect" in His sight before God accepts us into His family. Apart from the perfect righteousness of Jesus Christ

---

1. Spartanburg, S.C. *Herald-Journal*, December 17, 2005, p. B8. There are no capital letters in this title other than the word "God."

that God attributes to a believer, he is totally unacceptable. I suspect that Graham is thinking of works righteousness and the inability of a sinner to live a perfect life. But to fail to speak of the perfection that is in Christ as a necessary substitute for our failure, especially under the rubric of "acceptance," is not only misleading, it demeans our Lord and His work on our behalf. No one is acceptable apart from perfection in Christ. Third, while fellowship with other Christians can be profitable spiritually (and granted, this emphasis grows out of the question Graham's reader asked about church membership), nevertheless, it is the ministry of the Lord's Word, used by His Spirit, that causes spiritual growth.

The answer given by Graham accommodates the faith to acceptance theory, thereby minimizing (if not actually negating) both what has been called the "passive" and the "active" obedience of Christ. Passively, Jesus bore the punishment for the sins of His own, taking away their guilt. Actively, He lived a perfect life that God attributes to believers by faith so that, in His sight, they are reckoned perfect. To speak of "accepting us just the way we are," is misleading at best. Neither is the statement accurate when applied to a believer. It is this sort of fuzzy thinking and teaching that has confused many. The emphasis is upon man, not upon the work of Christ. When you detect it in the thinking of counselees, take the time to set the record straight!

CHAPTER SEVEN
Compassionate Teaching

Now, let's look again at one of the ways in which Jesus showed compassion. In Mark 6:34, we encounter what might at first seem an unnatural juxtaposition of ideas. Mark says that Jesus was moved with compassion "so He began to teach them many things." What does teaching have to do with compassion? How must we bring these two thoughts together?

Sheep without a shepherd are helpless, prey for wild animals. They are scattered and tend to wander off into briar bushes in which they may become entangled. They lose their way and cannot find the sheepfold. They need the guidance and care of a shepherd of the sort that is described in Psalm 23. Without such care they are a pitiful lot. It was sheep in that condition that moved Jesus to compassion.

But why "teach?" Because that is precisely what they needed and were not getting – they were without a teaching shepherd. When speaking about spiritual shepherding and sheep, teaching is the same as providing food and giving protection. The sheep need to be led into green pastures beside still waters where they can feed and rest. They need the protection of the rod and the staff that the shepherd carries with him.[1]

The shepherds of Israel, the prophets, priests and kings, throughout the years failed to provide what was necessary for the spiritual welfare of their people. Even a casual acquaintance with Jeremiah 23:1–4 and 50:6–7, in which God so plainly describes the deplorable condition of scattered sheep without a shepherd's guidance, makes these things clear (see also Ezekiel 34:2–6). Thoughts like those of the prophets must have run through Jesus' mind when he saw the people and was moved with compassion for them. The shepherds in His day were no better than those in former times. They had

---

1. See my book, *Using the Rod and the Staff.*

allowed the people to wander unattended. They were "lost" sheep (Matthew 10:6; 15:24).

The same thing is happening again today! People are confused. They wander like lost sheep from one religious TV program to another, they peruse the experience-oriented books that make the bestseller lists, they roam from one church to another – all in search of something more. Something that they ought to have been given by faithful shepherds. God's people have become prey for ecclesiastical shysters who are all too willing to lead them astray. Having been served pablum from their pulpits and heresy on TV, people are like weak, wandering sheep, not knowing the way to return to the Lord's fold.

It was this sort of thing that moved Jesus, in an act of compassion, to stop and teach the people. Doubtless, the uncertain teaching of scribes like Shammai and Hillel, who taught without authority (Matthew 7:28, 29), had left them with muddled minds: "One scribe says this, another that. Who is right?" They had been harassed by these hypocritical religious leaders who would not lift a finger to help them. Jesus offered refreshing teaching (Matthew 11:28–30), their teaching was onerous, legalistic, and wearing. The same is true of much teaching in the church today. Why is this?

Many churches are more anxious to gain members than to feed the ones they already have. Spiritually lean sheep, wasting away under shallow preaching, is one problem. Elders who are afraid to confront error and false teaching is another. People receive neither adequate provision nor protection from their shepherds. Sheep are not sustained throughout the week by superficial teaching when, no matter what the text may be, the sermon becomes another Gospel message. The Gospel is wonderful, but the sheep need more than the Gospel to grow strong. No wonder sheep wander, seeking something more substantial. The problem is, they don't know how to discern truth from error because they have never been taught to do so. So, they end up buying into all sorts of strange views.

Compassionate Teaching

The elders of the church, who are charged with using the rod and the staff to ward off vicious animals and keep sheep from falling off a precipice, have failed to fulfill their trust. They will not enforce church discipline, they allow every sort of literature to be distributed among members of the congregation, and they fail to identify and warn against error and deception.

Peter understood the dangers of inadequate teaching. He wrote about those who "twist" the Scriptures because they are "untaught and unstable" (II Peter 3:16). That is why he urged his readers to "be on guard" so that they "won't be led astray by the error of lawless persons and lose their own stability" (v. 17). He was being a faithful shepherd in writing this way. It is only to be deeply regretted that the congregation to which he wrote failed to heed his warning, as we have seen from the book of Jude which was directed to the same church. Indeed, they allowed the errorists into their midst with devastating effects that Jude likens to burning the church down around them! Lack of proper teaching leads to lack of stability which, in turn, leads to further erroneous teaching, and so on. People must be taught. For them not to be instructed as they should be means that they will be scattered like sheep without a shepherd. Ezekiel mentions a time when God Himself will undertake to shepherd His own, a prophecy that was fulfilled in Mark 6:34 (see Ezekiel 11:2; 34:11). Every pastor must never forget that teaching is an act of compassion, and must not allow his congregation to forget it either.

The word Mark used in 6:34 is *splagchnizo*, a term that focuses attention on physical effects within a person's body. It has to do with one's feelings being so disturbed that they grip him in the guts. When a counselor encounters a counselee who has gone astray because of poor shepherding, it ought to move him to pity and anger. This is a right reaction to such wanton neglect. It is evidence that there are shepherds who have failed him. Counselors *should* get "worked up" over shallow teaching and the teaching of error. If they don't, that indicates that there is something seriously wrong with their perception of their own shepherdly counseling task. Moreover, they should do what Jesus did – teach the truth their people lack.

Because of the flawed teaching that exists in the church, as a counselor you will find it necessary to teach even in counseling sessions. You should never assume more knowledge on the part of counselees than they possess. Continually check out what they understand before making an assignment. More often than not, you will discover that you must straighten them out theologically. You will find it necessary to explain passages that have been distorted (see the previous chapter in which it is noted how Matthew 7 has been misunderstood).

So compassion in counseling, among other things, means the teaching of truth to those who lack it and to those who have been deceived. Never forget this fact.

CHAPTER EIGHT

Another Side to Compassion in Teaching

I mentioned in passing the words of Christ in Matthew 11:28–30. It is now time to exposit and apply them. Here they are:

> Come to Me, all who labor and are heavily burdened, and I will refresh you[1] (v. 28).

These words introduce the passage. And they are most interesting and profound. First, the word "come" is a special term which indicates that the one who is speaking is at the same time motioning with his forefinger, bidding the listener to come to him. That means this is a strong, urgent invitation. Jesus is not only inviting men to come to Him, but is anxious to see them do so.

Second, Jesus is issuing the invitation to all those who are "heavily burdened." The burden He has in mind is not some physical load; it is the burden of sin that one carries about until he is relieved of it. It also included the heavy legalistic burdens that the scribes and the Pharisees placed upon the people. Jesus spoke of these in Matthew 23:4 when He said, "They tie together heavy loads and put them on people's shoulders." He was referring to the traditions of the fathers that went far beyond the biblical commands given by Moses. "And", He further observed, "they don't want to lift a finger to budge them" (v. 4). Their teaching crushed the hearts and souls of those under their care. And there was nothing in it of joy, peace, or "refreshment." There is much deadly teaching like that today in the church.

In contrast, in issuing His invitation to come to Him for teaching, He went on to say, "I am meek and humble in heart, and you will discover refreshment for your souls" (Matthew 11:29). There are two important facts in that statement. Again, Jesus mentions the refreshing character of His teach-

---

1. A more accurate translation than "give you rest" (KJV).

ing. It lifts the burdened and weary and enables them to carry on joyfully in the future. He not only knows man is but flesh, He also took on a fleshly body. Second, He mentions the compassionate nature of His own character as a teacher: "I am meek and humble in heart." He will not lord it over those whom He teaches. Rather, He will be helpful and not reproach those who are dull learners or who ask ignorant questions (cf. James 1:5). He will correct errors and teach truth in such a way that He relieves His students of unnecessary burdens. All of this is in direct contrast to the overbearing and burdensome teaching of the Pharisees.

Indeed, in concluding, He emphasizes the fact that His "yoke is easy to wear," and His "burden is light" (Matthew 11:30). How reassuring! Such teaching is refreshing, heartening, and not difficult to understand or heavy. And when it is obediently practiced, it is not difficult to do. What a graciously compassionate invitation it is!

Now, may I suggest from this passage that you should take away these two thoughts:

1. Biblical teaching is compassionate since it lightens one's load. There is nothing oppressive about it; when followed it adds a lilt to life.
2. Biblical teaching is compassionate because of the character of the One Who gave it to us. He is meek and lowly, He understands our infirmities, and He is working with us by His Spirit enables us both to will and to do those things that please Him (Philippians 2:13). His teaching is designed to lift the load of guilt from sin, and to help His disciples avoid it in the future. Unlike the scribes, he *does* lift a finger to help; indeed, when need be, He offers His whole hand!

Jesus shows compassion, then, in recognizing the need for lightening our load. That grows out of a feeling of pity and mercy for saved, but still struggling sinners. They need help in their quest to become like Him. There also is compassion behind the manner of His teaching. He knows our infirmities and our struggles, and pitches His teaching toward them. He

Another Side to Compassion in Teaching

also encourages those who fail and helps them to recoup from the failure. In other words, He shows the utmost compassion in every aspect of His teaching.

As counselors, we must learn to imitate Him in these things. We must be sure that our teaching lifts and refreshes the spirits of those we counsel. And we must be sure that we are never harsh or act as if we are "superior" to them. Probably, most instruction in colleges and seminaries (not to mention churches) is the very opposite of what Jesus, the perfect Teacher, taught us that Christian teaching should be like. It is time for Christian teachers to learn from Him Who bids them to put His yoke upon them.[1] Never fear; it is light. Counselor, is your teaching light?

---

1. To wear the yoke of a teacher in biblical times was to become his disciple (cf. Lamentations 3:27).

Chapter Nine
Are You Moved?

If not, something in you must change! Do you love God and your neighbors (in this case, specifically your counselees) enough to feel pity, extend mercy, and show compassion to them? Many are disagreeable, unlovely people, clearly not the sorts of persons you would choose for friends. They exhibit anything but loving attitudes themselves. Some exhibit behaviors that are downright deplorable. Other counselees are weak, untaught, full of fears and uncertainties. They have no stability and lack grounding in the faith. "Not the best of the crop," many would say. But they are the kinds of people to whom Jesus ministered!

When things go wrong for them, it would be easy to sit back in your chair and think (if not to say out loud), "You certainly deserve what you got!" Of course, that might be said properly – for instance, as a helpful explanation of what has transpired. But that isn't what I'm talking about. It's the exclamation point in that utterance which shows this wrong attitude. Or, it's possible to think or say, "I told you so!" (again, note the exclamation point). The attitude that those sentences exhibit is precisely what is wrong with much counseling – and counselors. *If that's the way you talk or think, then you must change.*

Rather than feel surprise, disgust, or satisfaction at the sin and suffering of a counselee, you must learn to maintain such a tender good will toward him that you genuinely feel sorry for him. When mishaps occur – as they often do – they should move you to compassion! You should sorrow with him, mourn over his sin and its consequences. You should truly "weep with those who weep." You must be *moved* by his plight – moved so strongly as to make every effort to help him, regardless of how repugnant his behavior has been. Indeed, when necessary, you must be willing to take even extreme measures to help him (remember the words of Jude).

What I am describing is a vital element in Nouthetic counseling compassion.

But most of all, as difficult as the temporal trouble that a counselee may experience, grief should well up within you as a biblical counselor (and as a fellow brother in Christ) over a counselee's trouble with God. It is not enough to feel and act with compassion because of the temporal plight of a counselee. As one who always ought to counsel from a vertical perspective, first and foremost, your emotional response ought to cause you to think (or say), "How sad it is that Marty has estranged himself from God!" In this case, the exclamation mark is most appropriate. Thus, thinking in these terms, your emotional response ought to be of a deep twofold nature. You should find yourself:

1. Grieving over the fact that God's Name and/or work has been injured by your counselee;
2. Grieving over the fact that the circumstance, if not changed, will inevitably lead to discipline from God.

It is important to keep both of these factors in view as you counsel. If the vertical dimension is missing, your counsel will be of no greater value than that which a non-biblical counselor down the street would give him. It is not enough to busy yourself with finding a remedy for a counselee's temporal troubles. Your motivation – not to speak of your emotional response – ought to far exceed that of other counselors. Your counseling is a ministry from God designed to bring honor to Him by helping His children solve problems His way, to His glory. You must have more than your counselee in mind.

"Ah," you say, "there is that ambiguous phrase, 'to God's glory.' What do you mean by that anyway?"

You're right. Often these words are used almost as a throw-away phrase that has little or no meaning, but sounds pious. But they are too important to be used in a meaningless manner. In contrast to those who do so, you must understand, and be able to articulate what you mean when you tell a counselee, "Do your homework this week to God's glory."

Are You Moved?

In the Scriptures, "glory" has two elementary meanings that Paul brought together in his phrase "the weight of glory" (II Corinthians 4:17). The Old Testament word for "glory" is *kabod*, which means "weight." The New Testament term is *doxa*, which means "fame" or "reputation." When a counselee glorifies God, he gives God His full weight, thereby spreading His fame or reputation. To give Him "weight" is to give Him credit for something good. biblical counselors, therefore, conceive of God as a "heavyweight" Whose honor must always be upheld as the force behind any good work that they do. They only "share" credit with God secondarily, as those who derive all the good they do from Him.

When God isn't glorified, man will rush in to take the credit. And others will be quick to give it to him. But God will not stand for that. Instead, He will so work out the circumstances of a case that, in the end, He *will* receive the glory – often at the expense of those who refused to give it to Him in the first place. But even that is compassionate since it provides opportunity and encouragement for those involved to repent.

So, counselor, there are wheels within wheels! And it is your privilege to sort them out for yourself and for your counselees. At times it may be difficult to demonstrate God's compassion in any given circumstance, but it is your task to articulate the principles of providence that enable one (often by faith) to declare He is present or at work. If you are not clear about the issue yourself, take the time to think through the matter of God's will in relationship to His compassionate actions. When you do, you will be able to help your counselee in ways that you could not before. Counselors who are properly *moved* compassionately are sorely needed. Can the church of Christ depend upon you to be one?

CHAPTER TEN
"How Do I Get it?"

"Did you say, 'Get it?' What are you talking about?" Yes, I said get it. Why are you counseling unless you already have it? What were your reasons for undertaking a counseling ministry in the first place? If you haven't "got it," perhaps it is because you *never* had it. If your motivation for becoming a Christian counselor was something less, or something other, than honoring God by helping His people when they are in need, then you may have entered the field under false pretenses. Or if not, under a serious misapprehension of what biblical counseling is all about.

"Get it? Get what?"

I am still discussing matters that were raised in the previous chapter – in particular, the emotional responses that ought to accompany and motivate a counselor when he discovers that God's Name is dishonored and His people are distressed (the latter, either as the result of the sinful actions of a counselee or his response to hurtful acts of others – or both).

"Well, I *was* wondering, as I read your discussion in the last chapter, how one might go about acquiring the emotional responses that you mentioned. I guess, to a large extent at least, it must be a part of his background. If it isn't there when he becomes a counselor, it would seem almost impossible to generate it. I suppose, for instance, that emotionally oriented persons are more likely to fit the mold you described. Isn't that so?"

No, not necessarily. Actually, emotion may get in the way. Indeed, such persons as those you are describing may find that *counseling* compassion is submerged under other emotions – those that are not aroused for proper reasons or manifested in proper ways. What God requires of all, all may have. It is not necessary to possess a particular sort of nature or background for a person to become compassionate.

What we have been talking about is not mercy, pity, or compassion that arises out of our natures or training, but

39

from theologically proper concerns for the honor of God and the welfare of others. Actually, these qualities must override much in the nature of every counselor. Emotionally oriented persons, for example, may find it difficult to separate their own natural responses from those that are biblically induced. Others may find it difficult to learn emotionally proper responses from those same theological understandings. At any rate, if you are one who has problems generating compassion toward others, in addition to asking God for help in doing so, ask yourself, "As a Christian counselor, on what do I focus?" By answering that question God may help you to see what must be done.

How may the question be answered? Remember that I am talking about focus – that area in which your deepest concerns lie. Let me suggest four areas upon which it is possible for you to focus. Your focus may be upon God, upon others, upon the counseling process, or upon yourself. Some consideration should be given to each of these matters, of course, but let me ask again where is your *focus*? That is to say, if you were to list these four areas in order of importance, what would the list look like?

If your concentration is on yourself, then it is entirely understandable that you may find it difficult to be *moved* with compassion for others. How can one who is always thinking, "What's in this for me?" become rightly concerned for others? How can one who worries about what people will think about him do the hard things that help? How can a counselor who is infatuated with success and accolades find compassion for others in his heart? I shall leave it to you to answer these questions.

If however, your concentration (or focus) is upon the counseling process and you are caught up in the theory and practice of counseling, you may be in danger of becoming an academic (believe it or not, there are some who find the thought enticing!). God and your counselee may easily fade into the background as you become more and more of a counseling buff. You may even approach the point where you

"How Do I Get it?"

become little more than a counseling theorist or a counseling mechanic! It is difficult to think of persons when you think principally about theories, methods, techniques, and systems. Such a focus puts persons – both human and Divine – much lower on one's list.

If your concentration is on the counselee, you may find it easier to become compassionate. Yet even so, the compassion you experience may be of a purely horizontal sort, in which God is omitted or shoved into the shadows. Such a failure is apparent when a counselor's uppermost concern is for the welfare and relief of his counselee.

Finally, if your concentration is *rightly focused* on God, you will discover that, rather than eliminate them, this fact brings the other three areas into proper focus. Yet even here, it is possible to adopt a cold, sterile theological deadness if you don't have a living, vital fellowship with God through His Word. If one studies about God and His will merely from the viewpoint of how to use the knowledge gained in counseling, this failure is likely to occur. Instead, he must first study for his own edification. Perhaps there is no way in which a counselor is more likely to deceive himself than in this matter. He must, therefore, be ever vigilant to be sure that this isn't happening to him.

True counseling motivation will come only to the one who puts God first in such a way that he will do whatever it is that the Scriptures require of him, regardless of the consequences. This "boldness" of which the New Testament speaks is denoted by the Greek term *parresia*. The noun means "willingness to speak without fear of consequences." It was for such "boldness" of speech that Paul and the other apostles prayed (see Ephesians 6:19, 20; Acts 4:29). When you read through the book of Acts, you discover that it was this boldness, more than any other trait, that characterizes the apostolic mission.

A biblical counselor with the right focus will not think primarily about bringing relief to his counselees. There are hardships that some of them will have to learn to bear. He will never ask the counselee to turn to quick fixes as some do, by moving away, avoiding people, getting a different job, taking a pill, etc. These ways of dealing with problems may enable one to temporarily escape pain and suffering, but have consequences that are unacceptable to God. A biblical counselor will be careful about advising such means of relief. But, on the other hand, he will not so concentrate on *what* he is doing in counseling or *how* he is doing it that he forgets those for whose sakes he is doing it.

So, what is basic to proper compassionate motivation? Simply (but profoundly) this: acquiring a love for God that transcends all else. As love for God increases, love for self will diminish. As love for God increases, proper love for others will increase. As love for God increases, a correct focus on the principles and practices of counseling will fall in line. Love for God is basic. So pursue it and, in time, other matters will come into clear focus.

Chapter Eleven
Jesus' Compassion

At this point in our study I want to stop and take a quick look at how Jesus showed compassion. It is prudent to do so because those instances in which His compassion is noted provide us with the largest number of scenarios in which we read of compassion in the Scriptures.

First, the terminology describing Jesus' compassion is significant. The word most often used to express His tender concern for others is the most visceral Greek word for compassion, *splagchnizomai*. This word, as we noted earlier, has been translated a number of ways, such as "moved within." But that is a euphemistic use of the term which, in reality, describes a pitying sensation felt in the bowels. The location of the feeling is identical to that experienced in the older elevators which, after descending rapidly, came to an abrupt stop. If you have ever experienced the sensation to which I am referring, you know what I mean. At any rate, that which it describes is an inner feeling of tenderness and pity that occurs within the viscera.

Two other terms used more generally of Jesus' compassion, found in Hebrews 4:15 and Hebrews 5:2 respectively, are *sympatheo* and *metriopatheo*. The former is akin to our word "sympathy," while the latter means "to feel pity in a measured way" (i.e., "moderately"). This more general use refers to the overall ministry of Jesus as one in which He is said to be a high priest Who is "able to *sympathize* with our weaknesses" (Hebrews 4:15), and Who is "able to *act gently* toward the ignorant and wayward since He Himself is inextricably involved in weakness" (Hebrews 5:2). In other words, we are led to understand that in becoming a man like us Jesus was able to experience the temptations and the difficulties that other human beings do (yet without sin). He is not removed from our plight. He can even understand how human weakness may make it easy to fall into sin and how ignorance can lead to iniquity. Remember, it was He Who said, "The spirit is willing, but the flesh is weak" (Matthew 26:41).

Because of His close identification with us – not forgetting that He never succumbed to these weaknesses – we can rejoice in the fact that He understands us and, therefore, sympathizes with and deals "moderately," or "gently" with us. These facts should be reassuring to people like us who, faced with similar temptations as Jesus, *have* fallen. Presumably, these weaker words are used, rather than the stronger *splagchnizomai* that we find all over the Gospel accounts, in order to describe Jesus' ministry as a whole. These less emphatic terms understandably contrast with those used to describe compassion in the actual situations in which Jesus responded to individual instances of need. The writer of Hebrews, it would seem, was far enough removed from the emotion of the moment that stirred Jesus to action on so many occasions, that it was possible for him to use such measured terminology. This would explain the more general, less emotional language that we find there.

It is good to know that Jesus felt (and feels) tenderly toward us – even when we are "ignorant and wayward." This knowledge is one of the lasting benefits of the description of His humanity in relationship to ours that is given in Hebrews. But as the author possibly did, to some extent we might have deduced this from the Gospel record itself. Nevertheless, it is helpful to have it spelled out in Hebrews in so many words!

In teaching about the miracles of Jesus, some have reduced what they read to an apologetic for His deity. Surely, that He is God is one large truth that we should glean from those accounts. But in doing so, too often the tenderness and the inner feelings that are described as "compassion," have been missed by those writers. We must remember that these miracles were not presented as cold and calculated events in which a blind man would be healed *merely* because that healing would give evidence of Who Jesus was. The evidential character of miracles stands out plainly According to John 9:3 and

Jesus' Compassion

also in Acts 2:22 and elsewhere. But we must turn to the miracles not only for their apologetic value; in them we also discover the extent of Jesus' tender concern for His fellow human beings. Those who are blind, crippled with illness, demon-possessed, and even those who had lost loved ones are said to be objects of His compassion.

Beyond these facts, as a second benefit from the study, we learn also that Jesus didn't always heal everyone that He might have. He often avoided the crowd when He was able to do so.[1] And He even urged those He did heal to be silent about the fact in order not to attract others (see Mark 1:44; 7:36). It seems that, as much as possible, He made a point of circumventing crowds. Why? For one reason, He was on a schedule. His brothers urged Him to go to Jerusalem where people could see the work that He [was] doing (John 7:3) in order that He might become famous. But He refused and went up secretly because, as He told them, "My time hasn't yet come" (vv. 6, 8, 10). He was following a Divine timetable. We can be certain that Jesus did nothing that would interfere with that schedule. Although it provided for much flexible time in which He could work miracles of compassion, the schedule would override doing so when they might interfere with it. That too is instructive.

Jesus helped some (actually he healed and otherwise helped *many*), but He could not be everywhere, helping all. As we just saw, He had other responsibilities to meet. So He carefully allotted time to healing, to preaching, to counseling His disciples, and to choosing those whom he would help. A counselor today must do the same. Once the word gets out that there is help to be had at such-and-such a church where biblical counseling is done, soon more people than it's possible to help will arrive on the doorstep. Doubtless, Jesus felt compassion for more people than he healed. A good counselor will as well, but having thought through his responsibilities, he

---

1. See, for instance, John 6:1–3. Because of the crowd that followed Him, Jesus left them and went up into a mountain to be alone with His disciples.

will not countermand good decisions made in times of thoughtful reflection by making spur-of-the-moment emotional commitments that he shouldn't.

Let's now look at a couple of the many instances in which Jesus *did* help people, out of compassion, to see what else we can learn from them. We read that after Jesus healed the man by the pool of Bethesda He said to him, "See, you are well again. Sin no more, or something worse may happen to you" (John 5:14). It's evident from this that He was as much concerned (if not more so) about the soul as about the body. We read that Jesus fed the multitude from the five barley loaves and two fish out of compassion (John 6:10). He also used the instance as a teaching tool shortly thereafter as He declared that He was the "Bread of life" (John 6:35). Once again we see, in close proximity, concern for both the physical and the spiritual sides of man. It is not necessary to mention other passages to substantiate this claim. The truth of it is apparent as one reads the Gospels. But it must not be missed. Jesus' compassion extended beyond the healing of His followers' bodies to their eternal welfare.

But there are those in Christian circles who will not evangelize (as Jesus did) or deal with the spiritual issues of believers in conjunction with their counseling practices. Various reasons are given, into which there is no need to enter here. The fundamental concept itself is what should concern us: they are willing to extricate persons from all sorts of temporal problems without making any attempt to deal with their souls. Of what profit is it to help people with their temporal problems and then dismiss them to continue on their way to eternal punishment without presenting the Gospel to them? The practice is askew. Though they would not classify themselves as theological liberals: nevertheless, their approach is no different from that of most classic liberals.

Such compromising counselors may claim that what they do is compassionate – and they think that's what counts. But their concept of compassion is limited to only one aspect of man's being and is surely misplaced. It was Jesus Who said,

"Life is more than food, and the body is more than clothing" (Luke 12:23). And He demonstrated what He taught by the compassion that He showed for the eternal welfare of those He helped. So it is important to be sure to undergird all temporal help that is given to counselees with spiritual help. This is a prime lesson to be learned from Jesus' ministry.

Chapter Twelve
Compassion isn't Optional

"I'm just not the compassionate type," you may object. Well it's true that you may not be. But that's merely telling us how things *are*, not how they *should* be. If what you say is true, you must learn to be compassionate.

"No, you just don't understand. I may be deficient, but compassion just isn't part of my personality."

OK. So it's not a part of your personality. But all that means is that you must change."

"Change? Change my personality? I've never heard of that before. Are you sure it's possible to do so?"

Of course it is. It happens all of the time. God turns nasty people into nice ones, angry persons into ardent ones. Think for a moment about Peter. If ever there was a vacillating, weak and impetuous person, it was he. Yet Jesus not only changed Simon's name to "Peter" (which means "rock"), He made him into a rock as well. The man who quivered at the accusation of a little servant girl was changed into the fearless preacher who said such things as "you killed the Author of life" (Acts 3:15) to the very persons who put Jesus to death. No, God can change a personality – even yours!

"Are you sure that I have to undergo such a change? Do I *have* to be compassionate?"

Well, let me read this from Colossians 3:12, and you tell me: "put on compassion, kindness, humility, meekness and patience." Now what do you think?

"Wow! From that verse, it looks as if I have a string of qualities to learn as well as compassion."

Perhaps so, but we'll begin with compassion.

"I can see it's a command – *put on* compassion – but I missed any reference to how I might do so."

First of all, you can see, can't you, that if it's a command, then it's possible to make the change.

"I'm not sure. How is that?"

You see, God never commands His people to do anything He doesn't provide the desire and the ability to do. That means you don't have to pull it off alone. Sure, you must obey the command – but by using the wisdom and the strength that He grants. Listen to this from Philippians 2:13: "It is God who is producing in you both the willingness and the ability to do the things that please Him." The Colossian 3:12 command is introduced with these words: "So then, as God's chosen people [all – not just some part of them], holy and dear, put on..." Since you belong to that group, the command is for you. And since the command is for you, God will grant you what you need to make the change. Got it?

"Uh...yes, I think I have. I'm one of the members of New Testament Israel, the Church, so I guess I'm included. But how do I go about pulling it off?"

To begin with, remember James 1:4–5. In speaking of a person who lacks wisdom, he says, "Let him ask God for it, since He gives to everyone unreservedly and without reproaching, and it will be given to him." Now, James happened to be talking about wisdom, in particular, but he also noted in passing that what he said is true of all of those things God commands. In verse 4 he says that God wants us to "be complete, lacking in nothing" (which would include compassion). The "complete," or spiritually well-rounded person, as the original word (*teleios*) indicates, is one who "has it *all* together." If you "lack" compassion, not only are you incomplete in that regard, but also God wants you to do something about it and will assist you in filling in the gap. What do you say?

"If that's the way it is, how can I say 'No?'"

You can't, and still please God. But your concern, I gather, is to know how to become a compassionate person. James says pray. That's the first step in the process. Second, at the end of the tenth chapter of this book, we saw how coming to love God and man is basic to learning compassion.

"Yes, but that only complicates matters. Now, I have to learn how to love as well as learn how to be compassionate."

Compassion isn't Optional

No, you don't. The two go together. As your love for God grows, your love for others will grow too. And as your love for others grows, so will compassion for them. Compassion is one aspect of love. I shall not spend much time discussing this matter but simply emphasize the fact that, as Jesus said (and Paul reiterated), coming to love another is a matter of *giving* him something that he *needs*. They both tell us that if your enemy hungers, you should feed him. If he is thirsty, you should give him a cup of cold water. And if he needs what you have, you should lend it to him (Luke 6:35; Romans 12:20). When you learn to love an enemy by giving to him, you will also learn to show compassion to him.

"Well, I guess that's the nub of it all. If I have trouble showing compassion, I must give what I have to begin meeting needs."

Right. That may mean time, effort, money – whatever – so long as he *needs* it and you *have* it. The way that you may begin this is by taking a deeper interest in people. Discover what their needs are. Otherwise, you will not be in a position to help them. In doing so, you will get to know people better, leave the isolation of your own comfortable world, and come to see how it is more blessed to give than to receive. There are few better ways to become better acquainted with a person than to seek out what it is that he needs and, if possible, provide it. When you invest yourself in him, you will grow closer and become more sensitive to him. As a result, when he is in trouble, you will discover compassion welling up within you. And in time, this approach will cause your compassion to broaden out toward others too. Love, clearly, is the answer you are looking for.

"Well. I think I understand. It's now only a matter of beginning."

Right. And remember, if love can be shown to an enemy, surely it can be shown to fellow-Christians in your church! That's a good place to begin.

CHAPTER THIRTEEN

The Good Samaritan

The greatest account of compassion told by Jesus is what has become known as the Story of the Good Samaritan and, therefore, deserves notice in this book. Let's look at it again in Luke 10:25–37:

> It happened that a certain lawyer stood up and tested Him saying, "Teacher, what must I do to inherit eternal life?"
>
> He replied, "What is written in the law? How do you read it?"
>
> And he responded, "You must love the Lord your God with your whole heart, with your whole soul, with your whole ability and with your whole mind, and your neighbor as yourself."
>
> Then He said to him, "You have answered correctly. Do this and you will live."
>
> But because he wanted to justify himself, he said to Jesus, "And who is my neighbor?"
>
> Jesus took up this question and answered:
>
> "A certain man was going down from Jerusalem to Jericho and ran into robbers who stripped and beat him and left him half dead. A priest who happened to be going down that road saw him and passed by on the other side. So too a Levite, when he came upon the place, saw him and passed by on the other side. But a certain Samaritan, as he traveled, came upon him, and was filled with pity when he saw him. So he went over to him, bound up his wounds and poured oil and wine on them. Then he put him on his own donkey, took him to the inn and cared for him. The next day, he took out two denarii and gave

them to the innkeeper and said, 'Take care of him. And whatever more you spend, I'll repay you when I return.'

Which one of these three do you think became the neighbor to the man who ran into the robbers?"

He said, "The one who showed mercy to him."

Then Jesus told him, "You go do the same thing yourself."

Now, there are many aspects of this story that might engage our attention, but for our purposes, we can mention only a few. To begin with, note the context in which the story is told. Here is a man, a scholar ("lawyer" means "one versed in the Law of Moses") who, as a theologian, ought to have known the answer to the question he posed. Whether he did or whether Jesus led him to it is irrelevant; the point that Luke makes is that he asked his question in order to "test" Jesus. He was interested in debating a theological issue with this new "teacher" (perhaps in order to "show Him up"). At any rate, Jesus pushed him to make the right response by His own questions. And when he did, Jesus agreed that what he had said is correct (v. 28). It is interesting that, rather than turning to the Ten Commandments, the lawyer quoted from Deuteronomy 6:5 and Leviticus 19:18, and Jesus approved of this. Perhaps this was a common summary of the Law at the time. At any rate, it gave Jesus the basis He wanted to expose the sin of this self-righteous, bigoted scholar. Jesus told him that if he did what the verses require he would have eternal life. The lawyer was not ignorant; he got the point – he would be unable to obey these absolute commands and would need forgiveness and a Savior in order to wipe out the sin of failing to do so. But for whatever sinful reasons, he didn't want to hear that. Instead, in order to "justify" his unwillingness to seriously consider Jesus' words, he asked another question that he thought would stump Jesus: "And who is my neighbor?"

The Good Samaritan

As an answer, Jesus told him the story of the compassionate Samaritan. Perhaps Jesus alluded to a priest and to a Levite in order to make it clear that being a religious leader no more justified one than if he were not. In the story a hated foreigner – a Samaritan – turned out to be the compassionate one. Indeed, out of mercy, he went to extremes to help the poor traveler who had come upon thieves. At any rate, it is apparent that Jesus' final response, "You go do the same thing yourself," was right on target and probably hit home (we don't know because the account ends there).

In the exchange it is crucial to note how Jesus construed the Leviticus passage. It says that one is to love his neighbor. But Jesus enlarged the meaning to say that the Samaritan himself – not the injured man – was the neighbor. He "became" a neighbor to him merely by coming across him on the road. In other words, any person in need might become one's neighbor, and therefore according to Leviticus 19:18, one to whom loving mercy and compassion should be shown.

That was a new concept to the theologian who, doubtless, had debated before about who in the verse quoted was the "neighbor." Jesus settled the matter for him – and for us – by explaining that we might become a neighbor to anyone in need.

Well, what can we learn from this incident?

Of prime importance is the fact that "as the occasion arises," we are to "do good things for all men, especially for the members of the household of faith" (Galatians 6:10). It is interesting that the Samaritan had no idea that the "occasion" would arise. What he did was unexpected. But he met the immediate need that God had placed before him. That is the form that compassion often takes – unplanned, immediate action. And this is an important lesson to remember.

Moreover, it is clear that (according to Paul) we must always make helping our fellow members in the faith a priority. If the choice is to be made between giving to the need of a family in the church or some other good cause, there should be no question about where the money should be spent.

Compassionate Counseling

While we must not limit the meeting of needs to believers, when there is a choice – and it is impossible to meet the needs of both – those of the members of the household of faith should come first. So, from this we learn that, while compassion often may be spontaneous, at the same time it may be regulated by the principle in Galatians 6:10.

Finally, from that verse, it is clear that it is not necessary for one to go about looking for needs (though if he lacks compassion, he might learn it from doing so[1]); those circumstances that providentially *come to him* are to be carefully considered. Note, Paul says, "As occasion arises." One cannot meet all needs, so those that God brings into one's purview ought to be the ones he considers.

---

1. Not, of course, by becoming a busybody. The needs that he seeks to discover ought to be apparent to anyone who is open to meeting them – as indeed, were those of the injured man to the Samaritan.

CHAPTER FOURTEEN

Compassion in Conflict

There was a growing split in the church at Philippi. Factions were headed by two women, Euodia and Syntyche (Philippians 4:2). Before mentioning the division, Paul is careful to stress the need for unity. From chapters 1:27–2:13, this is his one emphasis. There is no time to discuss the entire section here (if you wish, you may read my commentary on Philippians). The one factor that is of immediate concern to us is that, in calling for unity, Paul urged that compassion be shown (2:1). The word used in this connection is *oiktirmoi* (sometimes used with *splagchna* meaning "bowels of compassion," as it is here).

It is interesting to ask, "Who was it that Paul had in mind?" He says, "If there are any feelings of affection and compassion, then make my joy complete by thinking alike, having mutual love, being united in soul, thinking as one" (2:1, 2). It seems that Paul has himself in mind! If the women could only come to agree on the matters that separate them (we are not told what they were), then that would make Paul's joy complete (v. 2). It seems that he is saying, "Show some compassion toward me."

Perhaps, more readily than we can, Paul could make this appeal. This was his favorite congregation – the only one that he allowed to support him. He "had them in his heart," as he said (1:7). It must have been broken when he heard of the disturbance among them, and – added to this – he was in prison and about to appear for trial before Nero. His condition might, therefore, have made it altogether seemly for him to plead for feelings of compassion.

But is he thinking only of himself? In verses 3 and 4 we discover otherwise. There he sets forth three principles that, when followed, lead to unity. They are 1) to avoid selfishness, 2) to consider others better than one's self, and 3) to put the interests of others before one's own interests. Clearly, he is concerned about seeing these principles practiced at Philippi for the church's sake – not merely his own. And indeed, in these three principles, we see the outworking of "bowels of compassion."

How is that? Selfishness stands in the way of showing compassion. Whether it has to do with the selfish hoarding of funds, the selfish refusal to lend a hand to others in need, or the selfish way in which one spends his time and expends his energy on empty projects (Paul calls this "vanity"), it is clear that compassion can be stifled by selfishness.

In addition, humbly putting others first is a vital element of compassionate behavior. Remember that good Samaritan. He might well have considered himself better than that battered and beaten Jew, lying in the road. But he didn't. By what he did, he "put himself out" for another. That is a principal way of considering the welfare of another more important than one's own self.

And akin to the trait just mentioned, looking out for the interests of others is also at the heart of compassion. Were the women in question willing to follow these principles, fighting would have ceased and unity would have been restored. In other words, the elements of true compassion would have prevailed.

Of course, compassion for Paul and for one another is but half of the picture. Paul was also thinking of the congregation as a whole. Compassion among members is vital to a congregation's unity and productivity. Moreover, few things destroy the witness of a congregation more than internal battles among the members. So, God's Name needs to be brought into the equation as well. How often the world looks at a quarreling church and turns from Jesus Christ, its Head. Compassion toward Him, in honoring Him before others, is also to be considered.

Now, we need also to ask, is it proper for us to call on others to be compassionate toward us as Paul did? Certainly. What could possibly be wrong with properly asking someone to act as God wants him to? How (i.e., in what manner and spirit and for what purpose) it is asked, however, can be all-

Compassion in Conflict

important. To use the request as a weapon to thrash another is not acceptable ("*Your* problem is that you don't show enough compassion for me!"). At issue ought not be the compassion of the one who fails to show it but, rather, the genuine need of the one requesting it. The plea, as Paul's did, must come from a genuine need *for* compassion.

Just one final note on need. There are real needs, as we have noted throughout this book. But there are those who, in our time, have invented a new concept of need. The Need Theologians, as we might style them, no longer speak of a need *for* something (food, a vehicle to use for transportation, and the like); instead, they speak of "having a need to..." do something or other. The concept involved is psychologically oriented. It is as if one cannot control himself – "I had a need (an overwhelming inner urge) to do it." So when he wants to avoid responsibility for his actions, the subject of modern day need theology can always plead non-culpability: "After all, what could I do?"[1] I shall say no more about this than to urge you not to be taken in when you are berated for not showing a so-called "compassion" that is demanded to justify a counselee's sinful actions.

---

1. But God, though "compassionate and gracious," "will by no means leave the guilty unpunished" (Exodus 34:6, 7).

CHAPTER FIFTEEN

Philemon's Compassion

Though we do not know the outcome of this brief, but vital letter, we may be as assured of it as Paul himself was. Nevertheless, its study enlightens our understanding of compassion in more than one way.

First, let's recall the situation. Onesimus, a slave of Philemon, had run away. Somehow or other, in the meanwhile, he had become a Christian under Paul's ministry: "to whom I have given birth in my bonds" (v. 10).[1] Paul was in Rome, awaiting his trial before Nero, and Onesimus had become a great help to him. In those days, jails were not furnished with all the luxuries we find in some of them today. Indeed, even food and medical care had to be provided by friends of the inmates. Onesimus was one of those who ministered to Paul (v. 11, 13), and Paul was anxious to have him continue to do so. However, there was a problem; Onesimus was a runaway slave! What should Paul do about that? In verses 12 and following, Paul pours out his heart for the slave: "I am sending him back to you, though in doing so I send my very heart." Paul had become so dependant upon Onesimus' ministrations that it was like tearing out a part of himself in bidding him to return to Philemon. Yet without Philemon's "consent," Paul knew it would not be right to retain him.

So he sent Onesimus back to Philemon bearing this very letter. (The fact that we have it makes it clear that Onesimus didn't take this as an opportunity to flee, but actually delivered it in person. And because we possess it, we can safely assume that Philemon carried out Paul's request to free his slave to serve Paul.) But note what the letter says. In it Paul

---

1. This tender way of speaking of the conversion of someone under his ministry evidently was common among the apostles. John calls Gaius one of "my own children" (III John 4), and throughout his first letter, he refers to his readers as "little children" (in this instance, the reference may or not be to his own converts).

mentions several facts that lay a great deal of pressure on Philemon: I could have ordered you to free him (v. 8); I remind you that you owe your own conversion to my ministry (v. 19); I appeal to you to free him and send him because now, as an old man in prison, I need his help (v. 9); I know how well you have served others in the past, so I am confident you will in this also (v. 7); I will pay for anything he may have stolen (v. 18); You must think of him no longer as your slave, but as a "dear brother in Christ" (v. 16); I expect you to do even more than I suggest (v. 21); and finally, I am coming to see you as soon as I am set free (v. 22). The tone and the terms used are all a significant part of Paul's appeal.

From this little letter, we learn again that it isn't wrong to appeal to another to show compassion to us when there is a genuine need and when the one to whom we are appealing has the capacity to meet it. Moreover, we learn that it is not wrong to apply strong pressure – of the right sort – to bring about what we desire. While never insisting, Paul appeals to Philemon in the strongest, but tenderest of terms to show compassion on both him and Onesimus.

Nevertheless, we can see that because he wants the decision to be Philemon's own; Paul will appeal and persuade, but he will not coerce (v. 14). He recognizes the importance of allowing Philemon to show genuine compassion on his own. Otherwise, it would be of no benefit to him to do so. Moreover, Paul wants to see Philemon's compassion used as a means of extending the faith (v. 6). Throughout, although Paul shows concern for Onesimus and for himself, there runs the sub-theme of Paul's concern for the spiritual life of both master and slave and the work of the church. He knows how to put the two together in ways that are neither pious claptrap nor undue appeals made for materialistic ends. Paul is ever the true Christian in whatever he does or says when writing under inspiration.[1] What a wonderful example he sets for

---

1. Doubtless, since he was a sinner, he must have failed often as, indeed, we do. But here, he was writing by the Spirit of God, so that all he said and did was in accord with God's will.

Christian ministry to those who have the ability to show compassion! The letter ought to be used by pastors as a sample document to follow in such situations.

Note

The four small letters of the New Testament (II and III John, Jude, and Philemon) owe their brevity to the fact that each was dashed off and sent to deal with a pressing emergency. Each of these writers presents significant material in brief compass even though he could not at the moment go personally to those whom he was addressing or write at length about the issue. But because of the nature of circumstances, something had to be done right away. Hence, the letters were carried by the next available person traveling to the desired location (and this also may have been why they were so brief – there was no time to compose longer letters). Because of their brevity, sometimes they are neglected. But they contain truths that cannot be found elsewhere and thus ought to be studied as fully as any others.

CHAPTER SIXTEEN
How God Uses Compassion

Doubtless God uses everything for His glory. I am not about to claim some special place for compassion in His providential workings. But it is interesting to notice that it was compassion that led to the beginning, the survival, and the subsequent history of Moses and God's people. Note the following:

> Then the daughter of Pharoah came down to bathe at the Nile, with her maidens walking alongside the Nile; and she saw the basket among the reeds and sent her maid, and she brought it to her. When she opened it, she saw the child, and behold, the boy was crying. And she had pity on him and said, "This is one of the Hebrews' children" (Exodus 2:5-6).

The child, of course, was Moses. And anyone who knows anything about the beginnings of the nation of Israel and Moses' part in it understands the importance of this event at the Nile.

It is interesting how this scenario demonstrates the never-to-be-forgotten fact that one act of compassion can have much larger and more lasting effects than those that occur later on. The far-reaching implications of this act of compassion extend to the coming of Jesus Christ and to the salvation of all who put their trust in Him. If you have been saved by God's grace, it is correct to say that it was an act of compassion toward the baby Moses that made it possible. And it was through mercy, that went back to the days of Moses, that God bore with His rebellious people for many generations, as He tells us through Isaiah:

> For He said, "Surely, they are My people..." So He became their Savior....And the angel of His presence saved them; in His love and in His mercy He redeemed them; and He lifted them

and carried them all the days of old. But they rebelled and grieved His Holy Spirit; therefore, He turned Himself to become their enemy, He fought against them. Then His people remembered the days of old, of Moses... (Isaiah 63:8–11).

Note, also, how it was in the days of Isaiah when the people remembered God's mercy in the days of Moses that they repented of their sin, saying,:

> Look down from heaven, and see from Your holy and glorious habitation. Where are Your zeal and your mighty deeds? The stirrings of Your heart and Your compassion are restrained toward me. For You are our Father... (Isaiah 63:15, 16).

Mercy and compassion, from the outset, played a large part in God's dealings with Israel. The same, we can readily say, is true of His love and mercy shown toward His church in our time.

One manifestation of God's compassion for His people is found in the revelation of His constant concern for them throughout their long and troubled history. We read, "And the Lord, the God of their fathers, sent word to them again and again by His messengers because He had compassion on His people and on His dwelling place" (II Chronicles 36:15). Even until the very end, God's compassion continued. Through Zechariah, He put it this way: "Because I had compassion on them...they will be as though I had not rejected them" (Zechariah 10:6).

Sending His Word to them by His prophets is one of the principal ways in which God, in mercy, pity, and compassion, leads His own. But even then, in the face of great long-suffering on God's part, the history of His people has been to reject the "messengers" He sends. And this was ultimately what led to the downfall of Israel as a nation. Nothing could be clearer than this. For example, Jesus' parable of the workers in the vineyard is explicit (see Matthew 21:33–44). Even the Pharisees, usually so dense in their understanding, got the point of this parable (v. 45). The curious result was that, in spite of their understanding, they determined to arrest and kill Jesus – in fulfillment of the parable itself! There is no wonder that, when Jesus predicted the fall of Jerusalem in 70 AD, He summed it up this way: "Thus you testify against yourselves that you are the sons of those who murdered the prophets. Fill up the measure of your fathers" (Matthew 23:31, 32).

Even then, He was to extend His final appeal for forty years during which (referring to the apostles), He said, "I am sending prophets and wise men and scribes to you. But you will kill and crucify some of them...so that all the righteous blood that has been shed on earth...will come upon you...all these things will come upon this generation" (Matthew 23:34–36). Then, with great compassion of heart, Jesus cried out in anguish, "Jerusalem, Jerusalem, who kills the prophets... How often I have wanted to gather together your children as a hen gathers her young under her wings!" (v. 37). Here is the manifest mercy of God, crying out in compassion to the very end. Then comes this last bitter word: "But you didn't want Me to! See, your house is left desolate for you" (v. 37, 38). Except for the remnant that, under the preaching of the apostles, believed it was too late – the Spirit of God had left the temple. It was now "desolate." The shekinah glory was gone and there was written over it *Ichabod* ("the glory has departed").

The history of Israel was one of continued mercy and compassion from the birth of Moses, its founder, to the end. There is much to learn from this. That the Lord is long-suffering, slow to wrath, and full of compassion is one facet of the truth. But lest anyone should presume upon that goodness and mercy, as Israel did, it is important to remember that there is a time when God's compassion comes to an end. But for those who endure, there is this great assurance: "Surely goodness and mercy shall follow me all the days of my life, and I will dwell in the house of the Lord forever" (Psalm 23:6, NKJV)).

CHAPTER SEVENTEEN

When Compassion is Wrong

"Could compassion – this wonderful aspect of interpersonal relations – ever be wrong? From all we have seen thus far it would seem that compassion might fail to obtain desired results, may fall on deaf ears, and may be mistaken for something else, but that it might ever be wrong…? Hardly."

Ah! But there *are* times when compassion must be withheld, times when it would be *wrong* to show it.

"Can you tell me when?"

Yes. The short answer is: whenever God says it is wrong. The longer one – that discusses *when* this is – follows.

There were times when God told His servants the prophets He would show no compassion on His people. For instance, in II Chronicles 36:15–17, here is what the Chronicler wrote:

> And the Lord, the God of their fathers, sent word to them again and again by His messengers, because He had compassion on His people, and on His dwelling place; but they continually mocked the messengers of God, despised His words, and scoffed at His prophets, until the wrath of the Lord arose against His people, until there was no remedy. Therefore He brought up against them the king of the Chaldeans who slew their young men with the sword in the house of their sanctuary, and had no compassion on young man or virgin, old man or infirm; He gave them all into his hand.

Plainly, there comes a point when there is no longer a place for compassion. Notice, out of compassion, God sent messengers to call His people to repentance, but when they refused to heed them, He "brought up" the Babylonian army to slay all alike with "no compassion." Indeed, the point of His utter lack of compassion is made by mentioning various classes (young, virgin, old, infirm). In calling in Babylon to execute

His judgment upon Judah, God brought upon her a conquering king who had compassion on no one. There was a point in time when God's compassion came to an end.

Speaking of Israel, God said, "They are not a people of discernment, therefore, their Maker will not have compassion on them. And their Creator will not be gracious to them" (Isaiah 27:11). Clearly, in the destruction of Jerusalem, we encounter a time when God's compassion ran its course.

Again, He says, "I will not show pity nor be sorry nor have compassion that I should not destroy them" (Jeremiah 13:14). That is clear enough. Indeed, God said, "I shall give over Zedekiah king of Judah and his servants and the people" to Nebuchadnezzar who "will not spare them nor have pity or compassion" (Jeremiah 21:7). And it even came to this: "Do not enter a house of mourning, or go to lament or to console them: for I have withdrawn My peace from this people...My loving kindness and compassion" (Jeremiah 16:5). And finally, making reference to several Old Testament passages, the writer of Hebrews summarizes the way God treated specific individuals: "Somebody who has violated Moses' law dies without mercy on the testimony of two or three witnesses" (Hebrews 10:28).

Then there is the way in which God destroyed the nations who inhabited the land into which He was bringing Israel: "And you shall consume all the peoples whom the Lord your God will deliver to you; your eye shall not pity them" (Deuteronomy 7:16). They had filled up the cup of the wrath of God.

There is no doubt, then, that there are times when God did not show compassion, and times when He commanded His own people not to do so. But, note carefully, all of these were times when He was dealing with the people as a theocracy and times when, in His theocratic rule, He determined to bring judgment upon His people through the unmerciful actions of other nations. As the Ruler of the world, moreover, God would not allow His people to have compassion on the occupants of Canaan. These incidents (and they are not the only

When Compassion is Wrong

ones) have to do with God's theocratic justice and His general government of men.

So the question naturally occurs, "Is there ever a time when we, as individual Christians, should not pity others or show compassion to them?" The answer is, "only once." In New Testament times, when there is no longer an earthly theocracy, justice is left to the secular governing powers that exist (Romans 13:1). The church has no power to execute such judgment. Its power is purely ecclesiastical. That means the only punishment it may extend is excommunication from its ranks. It leaves all other matters to the state (Romans 12, 13).

But when the state, after a fair trial, determines punishment upon a criminal, whether it be the imposition of a fine, imprisonment, or death, it would be wrong for Christians – out of compassion – to protest. Note Paul's statement in Acts 25:11: "If, then, I were a wrongdoer, and had done something worthy of death, I wouldn't try to escape death." Unlike so many today who detest even the proper administration of justice, Christians recognize that it is wrong (and not compassionate) to show compassion toward those who make the community an unsafe place in which to live. Compassion, in such instances, ought to mean showing concern for those whom the perpetrator has injured.

A few years back, I was the chairman of a jury in California. There were two women on the jury who were avowed Christians. They were uncertain about finding the defendant guilty – even though the evidence was unmistakable. Their words kept exuding pity and mercy. They were manifestly wrong, and we showed them why. After much discussion, they agreed, and the accused was convicted. The fact is, their compassion was misplaced – they should have realized that they were doing the compassionate thing in locking him up so that he would not be able to prey upon others in the future. It might be stated as a principle that, *whenever an act is biblically compassionate, to do the opposite is to act in a way that cannot be compassionate.* That means you should always determine who it is for whom compassion should be shown.

And that can be determined only by biblical principles of justice.

"But what about repentance?" In matters of the Christian church, repentance is certainly a reason for showing compassion. In Corinth, upon Paul's orders, the incestuous man had been put out of the church. But he repented. Then, there were those who thought that his punishment should be continued afterwards. Lest there be no compassion felt, Paul wrote, "The punishment that the majority inflicted on this person is sufficient." And he went on to instruct the church that "instead of going on with that, you should rather forgive and help him, so that he won't be overwhelmed by too much pain" (II Corinthians 2:6–7). Clearly, there was compassion behind Paul's orders.[1]

So the rights belonging to the church are one thing; those belonging to the state are another. Acting as a member of a church, I had no right to accuse, judge, condemn, and pass judgment on the criminal in California. But acting on a jury, as an agent of the state, I did. That distinction is the one to keep in mind at all times when deciding whether or not to show compassion.

---

1. Incidentally, this man would have been excluded from the theocratic nation of Israel by death. Here, in the church of Christ, his penalty was exclusion by putting him out of the congregation.

Chapter Eighteen
When Compassion is Withheld

"OK. So there are times when it is right, indeed necessary, to withhold compassion. I can see that. But what about those times when it is wrongly withheld?"

That certainly, is the next logical question. Wrongly withholding compassion affects everyone negatively. It has negative effects on the one who needs compassionate treatment, on the one who fails to give it, and on the Lord and His church as a bad witness. Most seriously, it misrepresents God both to the world and to the church itself.

Perhaps the best place to begin to consider the matter is in I John 3:16–17 which reads:

> By this we come to know love, that He laid down His life for us; so too we ought to lay down our lives for our brothers. Now, whoever has the world's possessions and recognizes that his brother is in need, and stifles his emotions toward him, how does God's love remain in him?

Since it is true that Christians should go so far as to lay down their lives for one another, surely sharing one's worldly goods ought to be but a trifle. Yet few Christians seem to recognize the fact. Perhaps that is because they fail to understand what God's love requires of them. At any rate, let's look a bit at the passage.

It would seem apparent that if compassion for a brother in need moves us to do for him what is necessary to meet his need, we ought to follow the lead of our emotions in the matter. The ultimate sacrifice is required of few of us, but the lesser presents itself frequently to all of us. We should, therefore, fully understand what God expects of us.

Notice, it is the "stifling of emotions" (those feelings of compassion that well up when we recognize our brother's need) that inhibits action to meet needs and that demonstrates a lack of love for God and our brothers in Christ. John is speaking of the proper show of emotion that ought to impel all believers to bless others by showing mercy on those who are in financial difficulty. The original term he used is graphic: it speaks of "shutting up his bowels" toward a brother.

Paul speaks about being restrained *by* one's emotions in a similar passage (II Corinthians 6:11–12):

> We have spoken freely to you, Corinthians; we have had wide open hearts. You aren't being restrained by us; you are being restrained by your own emotions.

The word "emotions" here is also "bowels" (*splagchna*). It was the Corinthians' restrained emotions toward Paul and his fellow-workers that was the problem. He and his companions had opened their hearts to them, but they had closed theirs because of the influence of false teachers. They had been restrained by their emotions in that either they had mixed emotions or they were holding back their natural emotions toward the founder of their church. Either way, they did not allow their emotions to guide them in the matter. It is possible, then, that one's emotions may work against compassion. In both passages, their cramped emotions would not allow them free rein in meeting the needs of another. Emotion kept them from doing what they ought to do.

In the cases just mentioned, a brother in financial need and an apostle in need of encouragement from his former congregation were in view. How frequently we find similar situations in our churches today! "John's poor family has so little," we may acknowledge, but if we begin to feel compassion for him, we find that it is all too easy to restrain it. We turn our attention to something else and the emotion (bowels of compassion) subsides. It is easy to mean well and intend to do something to alleviate another's need, but if plans to take action are postponed, we may never get around to doing anything.

Take Paul's need for encouragement and assurance that the Corinthians were not going astray. Frequently, nothing is

When Compassion is Withheld

done to remedy the financial needs that many pastors have, but even more so, the sort of needs that Paul was experiencing. Some find fault, no matter what the pastor does or says. Others teeter on leaving the church for some foolish, inconsequential reason such as the color of drapes at the windows. Pastors feel it deeply when their ministry goes unappreciated – just as Paul did. Ordinarily, it isn't because they want recognition, but they want to see the positive effect of their ministries taking hold in the lives of the members of their congregations. Sometimes, there is even a need for a pastor's family to be accepted socially by the congregation. "I'd like to have them over for a meal, but they have four children. It would be a lot of trouble and expense to do so. I know they'd probably be happy to come, but…" Need more be said?

Whatever the circumstances, when one feels compassionate feelings welling up within, he ought to give heed to them. Rather than stifling or restraining them, he should give full consideration to whether or not they have arisen for legitimate reasons, and what action (if any) they are indicating he should take. Having done so, if for biblically conclusive reasons he believes his emotions are not well-founded, he should refrain from taking the proposed action. The Bible, not emotions, ought to govern our decisions and actions. But if he recognizes that behind the emotions is some biblically legitimate reason for compassion, he must show it concretely. You might think of it this way: emotions may give rise to the issue, but the Bible decides it. He must never stifle any such strong motivation that arises from his understanding of Scripture.

CHAPTER NINETEEN

Compassion for Those Who Minister

In the last chapter I mentioned briefly the need that preachers – like Paul himself – have for encouragement given in compassion. There is one outstanding case in the New Testament where we see this at work. Here is what Paul wrote to the Corinthian church about his principal companion in the ministry, Timothy:

> Now, when Timothy comes, see to it that he has no reason to be afraid when he is with you, since he is doing the Lord's work just as I am. Don't let anybody make light of him, but provide what he needs to send him ahead in peace, so that he may come to me; I am expecting him with the brothers (I Corinthians 16:10, 11).

Now, Timothy was a young man who, it seems, was somewhat timid and fearful. We gather that from Paul's exhortations to him not to allow "anybody to despise your [his] youth" (I Timothy 4:12), and to remember to "rekindle into a flame God's gift... because God didn't give a spirit of cowardice, but of power and of love and of self-restraint." And he concluded by saying, "So then, don't be ashamed of the testimony of our Lord or of me His prisoner (II Timothy 1:6–8).

These words indicate a concern for Timothy's welfare. Paul obviously had compassion on this young man to whom he was preparing to hand the torch when he was put to death. Evidently, because of his youth, Timothy was hesitant to step forward. We can understand this when we recognize that he traveled with and ministered under the authority of the great Apostle Paul. Nevertheless, it was time for him to come into his own, and Paul knew it. So both by direct encouragement – as we see in the quotations above – and by preparing others to care for him, Paul was attempting to help Timothy to make the transition.

It would not be easy to take over the ministry. While Paul did what he could to make it a smooth transition, he clearly sets forth, in vivid detail, what Timothy would be facing (see II Timothy 3:1–9). But he doesn't merely do so. At the same time he reminds Timothy that he has been in training: "You, however [in contrast to those who would be deceived and fail (II Timothy 3:13)], must continue in those things that you learned and are convinced of, knowing from whom you learned them" (II Timothy 3:14). He was referring to the ministry of the apostles with whom Timothy had worked, Paul being the chief one. He had heard and learned the apostolic message and watched their method. And chiefly, Paul went on to remind Timothy that he knew "the sacred Scriptures" (v. 15) which contained the words of life, and that would be able to give him all he needed for his ministry of changing people (vv. 16, 17). The Old Testament Scriptures, along with the apostolic message (which currently was being penned as the New Testament equivalent) would be sufficient for his ministry.

Now, we can see from these passages that here was a man who needed compassion from an older minister and from the church that he served. He would get it by direction, by concrete travel help, by proper attitudes exhibited toward him, by exhortation, and under God, by direction from the Scriptures as his complete source of help.

Paul could see the need for all of these things in Timothy's life. And he was not about to see them neglected. As well as addressing two powerful letters about the work of the ministry to him, in which he provided so much direction, so much insight, and so much practical help, he also attempted to rally the churches behind him. Timothy was a young man, but as Paul reminded the Corinthians, he was in the same ministry as Paul and was to be respected for his calling and work in the Lord. No one was to "despise" him because of his youth. The word "despise" is, literally, "think down" or denigrate what he had to say to a lower level than what Paul said. And surely, what he told Titus would have applied too: "Let nobody disregard you" (Titus 2:15). Here the word "disregard" is, literally, "think around" which means to let what Titus said "go in one ear and out the other" – as we say today.

So, ministers – possibly some you know – could also use compassionate words, money, provisions, and the like from time to time, both from other ministers and from congregations. It doesn't matter into which of these categories you may fall. Take heed!

Chapter Twenty
Compassion for Brothers in Extremities

The Jewish Christians to whom the book of Hebrews was written had undergone severe trials for their faith. As the writer put it: "Now remember the former days when, after you were enlightened, you endured great battles with suffering" (Hebrews 10:32). And he continued: "you had compassion on those in bonds and you accepted the seizure of your possessions with joy, knowing that you have a better possession that is left" (v. 34). But as he wrote, they were on the verge of going back to Judaism. So the thesis of this book is to remember and compare what they now had with what they left behind. The point being that what they have in Christ is far better ("better" is a key word in Hebrews). Once they knew and believed this, but now they were allowing trials to wear them down.

The suffering had been great, but it had not yet extended to the shedding of their blood (Hebrews 12:4). There are warnings throughout the book (see especially, chapters 6, 10), but it is also filled with encouragement. Now, as encouragement, the writer urges his readers to "remember." In the former days, they were excited about their newfound faith. But since they had not fortified their thinking by the study and application of the Scriptures, they had become "dull of hearing" (Hebrews 5:11–14). This is always a possibility. Indeed, we ought to consider it a likelihood – when one fails to train his "perceptual faculties by practice to distinguish good from evil." They needed reminders of the past when they knew better. The neglect was unnecessary and, as a result, God was punishing them as sons (Hebrews 12:7–11). God's discipline was at work in their lives to purify and strengthen them. At one time, they understood this and even rejoiced in the trials that they had to endure for their faith.

When they were still spiritually strong, they were solicitous for one another. Some had been thrown into prison for their faith, and the rest "had compassion" for them (Hebrews

10:34). Precisely what this entailed we are not told, but we can be sure that it made a financial strain upon members who, themselves, were being dispossessed of their property, possessions, and funds. We know of the poverty of the Jerusalem church from the offering that Paul took up among the Gentile churches to meet their needs (another act of compassion on his part and on the part of Christians in Thessalonica, Corinth, and elsewhere). Their suffering brothers and sisters were in trouble, and these Gentile churches must help. So out of their own lack, they did what they could for those who lacked even more (remember what prisons were like in those days).

In this country, we have not yet reached the point where believers are thrown in jail for their faith as they are in China, Islamic countries, and elsewhere. In those places, where the need of all is great, we can be sure that there are those among their brothers who, like the Hebrews, will minister to them. When the opportunity affords itself, we who have so much also ought to do our part for brothers in trials like those the Hebrews were facing.

But even here at home, there are those who suffer for their faith. They may lose friends or jobs, be passed over at work, be scandalized, and so forth. Though most do not suffer as fully as those in Palestine did at the time the book of Hebrews was written, there are some who find themselves in dire straits. True compassion will not allow us to neglect or avoid our obligations to them. Toward the end of the letter, the writer of Hebrews again takes up the plight of prisoners: "Remember prisoners as if you were in prison with them and those who are ill-treated, as persons who also have bodies" (Hebrews 13:3). What a powerful appeal for compassion that is!

"Remember" – that is to say, "Do what you used to do for prisoners." Think of what it would be like to be there in a cell with them (and as a result, feel compassion for them). Think of the various types of ill-treatment that they suffer for the faith. If you put yourself in the place of those who suffer such

Compassion for Brothers in Extremities

things, your heart must go out to them. And then – in a startling final appeal – the writer reminds his readers that you are "persons who also have bodies" (v. 3). If that doesn't reach into the soul and stir the cold hearts of those who are sitting in comfort at home taking it easy, nothing will!

We too ought to do what is necessary today to help those brothers who are in some extremity. When we hear about it, we should not stop our ears, turn away, or change the subject. We should inquire into the situation, and if we deem that there is a biblically legitimate reason to help,[1] we must untie our purse strings or do whatever else is indicated.

Even in our day and in our country, there are brothers who are suffering for their faith. As Hebrews says, they might not yet be suffering by shedding their blood, but they are still worthy of caring compassion.

In counseling, do you open your wallet from time to time to help counselees in need? Do you urge counselees to help others? Does showing compassion play a part in your counseling as the result of allowing your emotions free reign? Do you also instruct, encourage, and exhort counselees to show compassion in biblical ways? How does compassion impact your day-by-day counseling sessions?

---

1. Fraud abounds, particularly in charitable appeals. Christians have a duty to use their (God's) money wisely, and should not give to all whose appeals come daily in the mail. Rather, after careful inquiry into appeals, they must choose those that seem legitimate and especially those that are urgent.

Chapter Twenty-one
The Cost of Compassion

Compassion costs! If it isn't time, energy, convenience, or interest that it costs, it's money. While money isn't the only factor involved in showing compassion to others, it plays an important part. So, it will be our primary concern in this chapter.

People donate to charities, Christians give to missionary agencies that feed and clothe persons in poverty-stricken countries, thousands of food baskets are filled and distributed to needy families, and other appeals for funds may be regularly found in the mail. Causes of every sort – some worthy, some not – attempt to tug at the heartstrings. It is, therefore, important for Christians to think and act when giving, in ways that please the Lord. And there is only one way that we can determine the principles for giving – from the study of the Scriptures.

Now, while there are other biblical principles involved in finances, we shall mention only those that pertain to compassionate giving. The first has to do with the giver, the second has to do with the cause, and the third has to do with the administration of funds. Who gives and how, why he gives to whom, and how the money is handled are all issues of significance. It is these three that I intend to consider in this chapter.

Biblical principles regarding the first of these matters may be found in II Corinthians:

> We want you to know, brothers, about the help that God gave to the Macedonian churches; how in much testing by affliction, their abundant joy and their abject poverty overflowed in a wealth of liberality on their part. I testify that they gave voluntarily according to their means, and beyond their means, earnestly begging us for the privilege of taking part in this service to the saints. They did this, not simply as we had expected, but

> first gave themselves to the Lord and to us by God's will (8:1–5).
>
> I don't want to relieve others by afflicting you; rather, it is equality that I seek. Your present abundance must be used to help those who lack in order that their abundance may supply your future lack, so that there may be equality in sharing (8:13–14).
>
> Now let me say this: "He who sows sparingly also will reap sparingly; he who sows bountifully also will reap bountifully." Each one must do what he has intended in his heart, not grudgingly or under compulsion, since God loves a cheerful giver. God is able to give you more than enough of every sort of gift that you may always have enough of everything to abound in every good deed. As it is written, "He scattered, he gave to the poor; his righteousness continues forever." The One Who provides seed for the sower and bread for food also will increase your seed and will enlarge the harvest of your righteousness. You will be enriched in every way so that you can engage in all sorts of liberality that through us will result in thanksgiving to God. The service that you perform by this religious function not only meets the needs of the saints, but it also results in many thanksgivings offered to God (9:6–12).

Now, it would be possible to do a detailed exegesis of these verses, but that is unnecessary. A straightforward reading of them itself makes the points that need to be made. I shall merely list some of those. Giving should be liberal. Such giving begins by giving of one's self to the Lord. Presumably, this means that nothing we are or have should be withheld when the Lord's people have need of it. Though the members of the churches of Macedonia had little themselves to give, they

The Cost of Compassion

gave far more to the needs of the poor at Jerusalem than anyone could have expected. Paul encouraged the Corinthian church to do the same. They had much, and they could give much. Paul did not intend to impoverish anyone; he wanted all to give equally. That, it would seem, is equality of percentage, not of exact sums. So too, as he says, when we give we should remember that God returns even more than we could possibly give. But when He gives, He does so expecting us to use it to help others.

The set of verses that pertains to the second factor in giving is Romans 12:13; 15:25–27:

> Share in meeting the saints' needs; pursue hospitality.

> But now I am going to Jerusalem to serve the saints, because Macedonia and Achaia have been pleased to make a contribution to the poor saints in Jerusalem. They were pleased to do so, and they are debtors to them. If the Gentiles have shared their spiritual things, they ought to be of service to them in material things.

Here Paul sets forth the cause. He makes two points: 1) the need is real and 2) the saints at Jerusalem have been impoverished for the sake of their faith. As we read in Hebrews, some had been dispossessed, others thrown in jail. Their wares were boycotted and they were excluded from the synagogues and other public functions. Because the Gospel "went out from Zion" (Isaiah 2:3), the spiritual blessing that went to the Gentiles certainly gave reason to expect at the very least a material return. So, Paul has made the case that the need is genuine.

Finally, in regard to the third principle, consider I Corinthians 16:3, 4 and II Corinthians 8:16–21:

> When I arrive, whoever you have approved I shall send with written credentials, to carry your gift to Jerusalem. And if it seems advisable for me to go too, they may go with me.

But thanks be to God for putting the same earnest concern for you in Titus' heart, because he welcomed our appeal and has such earnest concern for you that he is coming to you on his own accord. Together with him we are sending the brother who is well thought of throughout all the churches for his part in the furthering of the good news. And not only that, but he also has been selected by the churches to accompany us in the gathering of this charitable collection in which we are serving as administrators for the Lord's own glory and to show our eagerness. What we want to avoid is for anyone to be able to criticize the service that we are rendering in collecting this abundant gift, so we plan ahead to do well not only in the Lord's sight, but also in the sight of people.

It is plain that the sort of financial hanky-panky that has been exposed in recent days among televangelists and others was also a problem in Paul's day. Rather than have the Lord or anyone else criticize him or the collection, he planned carefully in advance ways and means of avoiding any accusations. His method – since the transfer of money in his time was by actual, physical means – was to have people accompany the money and see to its distribution. These were people chosen by the churches and certified by letter from them. It would be good if church organizations were as responsible today!

Now, there is a well-known parable that illustrates the principles above. It is, of course, Jesus' parable of the Good Samaritan. He was challenged by a genuine need – a man robbed, seriously injured, and left for dead on the road. Though inconvenienced, he stopped, took time to give physical help, dispensed oil and wine out of his larder, acted in concrete ways to see that the injured man would be cared for, and personally paid for this out of his own pocket. In addition, he promised to return to look further after his well-being.

Among other things, Jesus surely wanted us to see what genuine compassion costs.

Yes, compassion is more than good feelings, sympathy, or empathy as we noted several chapters back. It involves reaching deeply into the pocket, going the extra mile, and "putting one's self out" for the sake of others. Anything less cannot be called Christian compassion. Once again, counselor, let me ask you, "When was the last time you dealt with such matters in counseling?"

CHAPTER TWENTY-TWO
Compassion for Animals?

Last week Betty Jane, my wife, looked out the door and saw a beautiful white cat curled up on a mat on our back porch. We live out in the boonies of South Carolina, and from time to time, people come out from town and drop off animals that they either don't want anymore or can't care for. Now, we already had a cat and a dog (who on his own, as a puppy, wandered in a year and a half ago[1]). Now, I wasn't too happy to think of a second cat, but he (or is it a she? So far, it's hard to tell which with the full coat of fur *it* has) did look pitiful. He looked a bit bony, was crying for mercy, so...what else could we do? You're right, we took him in. Compassion – perhaps over wisdom – prevailed!

Now, as I thought of what we were getting into, I couldn't help remembering Proverbs 12:10: "A righteous man has regard for the life of his beast, but the compassion of the wicked is cruel."

I also remembered what God said to Jonah: "And should I not have compassion on Nineveh... in which there are more than 120,000 persons... *as well as many animals?* "(Emphasis mine; 4:11).

In these two verses, we see that compassion ought to be shown not only to human beings, but to animals. While there is no reason to join some animal rights organization or, go out in boats to save the whales because of these verses; nevertheless, the matter of proper animal care ought to be considered by every Christian. Too often in our discussions, the place of animals is simply ignored. (When was the last sermon you

---

1. Understandably, when our neighbor came looking for him (*he* was a he), she said she'd be more than happy if we kept him since he was one of a litter of nine. What was interesting was to see that she had compassion enough on this little puppy to come to our door asking for him. She might have simply said, "Glad to get rid of one. I wish the rest would walk off too!" But she didn't. We agreed to keep him since the dog we previously had disappeared just a month or two before.

heard about compassion to animals from a Bible-believing pulpit?) God has no problem with the killing and eating of animals for food and for sacrifice, nevertheless, while they are in our care, we must have compassion. Cock-fighting, for instance, in which the object of those who participate in it is to "enjoy" a bloody battle in which one cock kills another, is an example of the sort of cruelty mentioned in Proverbs 12:10. Merciless treatment of one's animals is forbidden and, indeed, condemned as "wickedness." This ought to be taken to heart by believers.

Now, it wasn't necessary for us to "take in" this cat, but, pity prevailed and we are "stuck" with it. Now that we have determined to do so, we must act responsibly toward it. We are not responsible for adopting every stray cat that appears on the scene, but if and when we do – and assume responsibility for it – we are obligated to show it "regard" (care).

It is of interest that, when speaking about having compassion for the people of Nineveh, God shows regard for the "many animals" in the city that would be destroyed if Jonah failed to bring the message of repentance to it. One would not have anticipated that, but there it is! I don't wish to prolong this chapter, or make more of this matter than I ought, but in studying compassion, it seems that the care of animals may not be avoided.

Just one more word. In terms of counseling there may be some benefit from considering the issue. If from his words (or those of his wife), a counselor detects a cruel attitude that a counselee has toward his pets ("He kicked the dog down the steps"), it might very well be the clue he needs to understand the kind of person he is counseling. If the counselee treats his animals that way, it is altogether possible that he could have something of the same attitude toward people as well – even if he doesn't actually "kick" them around physically! Is he an angry or even cruel person? At any rate, it might be well to investigate such matters.

CHAPTER TWENTY-THREE

What Compassion Does for Counseling

In Chapter Two I asked the question: "How is the counselor able to keep his composure" and to endure the wickedness that he encounters in counseling?" At that place I suggested that showing compassion was what made it possible. And I promised that, throughout the book, I would enlarge on that answer. Have you learned how compassion for others makes this possible? If not, let me go over it again.

When a person truly loves God and his neighbor, he will find it possible to counsel even the vilest persons imaginable. That is not to say that he does so without disgust, without proper judgment, or without trepidation. Yet, love *gives*, as it did when God loved us in spite of the fact that we were His enemies. If we love, we can show compassion. It is possible because we care about God's Name. We counsel His people so that they will be able to represent Him properly before the world. We counsel His people because we see how terrible the effects of sin are in the lives of those we are called upon to help. Love makes it possible for our hearts to go out to them.

But there are times when we may find it difficult to feel pity or mercy. Yet at those times, whether we feel like it or not, we can love because love is giving. We've seen that we can always give and, by giving, develop an interest in those in whom we invest our time, our energy, and our prayers. It is difficult to become wrapped up in the welfare of another (not to mention concern for God's good Name) without beginning to feel some kinship to that erring brother or sister that will develop into compassion. Just as compassion moves us to action, there are times when action moves us to compassion!

So as I have insisted throughout this book, there is no excuse for a counselor to be cold, uninviting, and aloof. He may find himself beginning to be that way, but the attitude should not last for long. Indeed, there is never an excuse for having to *develop* compassion for a counselee. The more we understand the Word of God and what it says about sin and

Compassionate Counseling

its consequences, the more we ought to be able to feel compassion for anyone who is caught in one of the strands of sin's web.

Yet, we too are sinners and need to be exhorted from time to time about our lack of compassion. If there is no one who can do this for you, you may need to refer to this book now and then as a reminder of the importance of compassion in counseling. It is too easy to become purely matter-of-fact in a mechanical way after having one's senses dulled by so much trouble and woe. One can become hardened by this, just as a physician might. There are those who speak of patients impersonally: "The gall bladder in room #456." A counselor may think of a couple as, "that marriage problem I deal with on Thursdays." If you ever catch yourself saying something like that, then rein yourself in and take time to reconsider your attitudes. While there are always times when, as sinners, we fail to measure up to the biblical ideals, we ought always to become conscious of this and rectify the situation forthwith! A counselor cannot counsel biblically by merely "going through the motions." He must "fill out" and punctuate his routine approach with mercy and pity. He is dealing with persons (God and counselees); not with inanimate objects or badly functioning machines. All such dealings are, necessarily, relational. One's relationship to God will affect his relationship to his counselees. His relationship to his counselees, conversely, will affect his relationship to God. God is not pleased with cold, hard approaches to counselees. He shows compassion to the fallen and He expects us to do so as well. After all, we ourselves have experienced His compassion in Christ. And when we look into the depths of our hearts and into the record of our past, we see how much wickedness that God, out of compassion, has forgiven us in His Son. In the end it comes down to this: we are able to be compassionate to others because of the compassion He has shown us in Jesus Christ.